YOU

BELONG

HERE

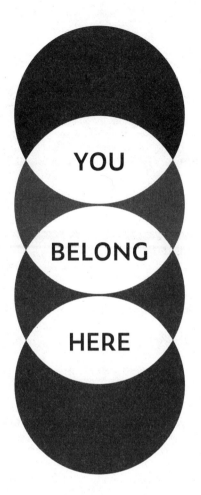

YOU

BELONG

HERE

The Power of Being Seen, Heard, and Valued on Your Own Terms

Kim Dabbs

Berrett–Koehler Publishers, Inc.

Berrett-Koehler Publishers, Inc.
1333 Broadway, Suite 1000, Oakland, CA 94612-1921
Tel: (510) 817-2277; Fax: (510) 817-2278; www.bkconnection.com

ORDERING INFORMATION

Quantity sales. Special discounts are available on quantity purchases by corporations,
associations, and others. For details, contact the "Special Sales Department" at the Berrett-
Koehler address above.

Individual sales. Berrett-Koehler publications are available through most bookstores. They
can also be ordered directly from Berrett-Koehler: Tel: (800) 929-2929; Fax: (802) 864-7626;
www.bkconnection.com.

Orders for college textbook / course adoption use. Please contact Berrett-Koehler: Tel: (800)
929-2929; Fax: (802) 864-7626.

Distributed to the US trade and internationally by Penguin Random House Publisher Services.

Berrett-Koehler and the BK logo are registered trademarks of Berrett-Koehler Publishers, Inc.

Printed in Canada

Berrett-Koehler books are printed on long-lasting acid-free paper. When it is available, we
choose paper that has been manufactured by environmentally responsible processes. These
may include using trees grown in sustainable forests, incorporating recycled paper, minimizing
chlorine in bleaching, or recycling the energy produced at the paper mill.

Library of Congress Cataloging-in-Publication Data

Names: Dabbs, Kim, author.
Title: You belong here : the power of being seen, heard, and valued on your own terms / Kim
    Dabbs.
Description: First edition. | Oakland, CA : Berrett-Koehler Publishers, Inc., [2024] | Includes
    bibliographical references and index.
Identifiers: LCCN 2023034729 (print) | LCCN 2023034730 (ebook) | ISBN 9781523005895
    (paperback) | ISBN 9781523005901 (pdf) | ISBN 9781523005918 (epub)
Subjects: LCSH: Self-perception. | Self-consciousness (Awareness) | Identity (Psychology) |
    Group identity. | Social psychology.
Classification: LCC BF697.5.S43 D325 2024 (print) | LCC BF697.5.S43 (ebook) | DDC
    158.1—dc23/eng/20231109
LC record available at https://lccn.loc.gov/2023034729
LC ebook record available at https://lccn.loc.gov/2023034730

First Edition

31 30 29 28 27 26 25 24 23 | 10 9 8 7 6 5 4 3 2 1

Book producer and designer: BookMatters
Cover designer: Marlon Rigel

To Steve, Micah, Henry, and Olive...

I am fighting for you.

CONTENTS

Introduction: The Journey to Belonging   1

1   We Are All Outsiders   13

2   Belong to Yourself   29

3   Your Four Identities   43

4   Lived Identity   51

5   Origin Stories   61

6   Learned Identity   71

7   Guiding Principles   89

8   Lingering Identity   101

9   Sunset Old Stories   113

10   Loved Identity   125

11   Build a New Table   141

Conclusion: Come as You Are   153

Discussion Guide   157

Notes   164

Recommended Reading   169

Acknowledgments   171

Index   173

About the Author   179

About To Belonging   182

BE • LONG • ING

BE is to exist.

LONG is the desire.

ING is the continual action.

Each of us are actively longing to exist.

Belonging begins with the individual.

Belonging begins with *you*.

INTRODUCTION

The Journey to Belonging

Stranger: Where are you from?

Me: Michigan.

Stranger: But you don't look American! Are you Chinese?

Me: No.

Stranger: But your face looks Chinese. You weren't born here.

Me: I was born in Korea.

Stranger: You must have come here for school?

Me: No.

Stranger: Well, then are you here because of your mother and father?

Yes, stranger. Thank you, mother and father, for leaving me on the street in a police box in Korea when I was six months old so I can explain this to a random taxi driver outside the Philadelphia airport.

• • • •

I've always felt the world was made up of places I didn't belong. As a Korean-born American adoptee who lives in Germany, Koreans often tell me that I'm too American. Americans tell me I'm too Korean. And Germans tell me I'm, well, I'm not German. Everywhere I go, they remind me I'm not one of them. I'm like the hot potato of inclusion. When you add in other aspects of my identity—female executive, community advocate, and mother—the plot thickens. The exclusion goes from overt to covert. It runs deep. No matter where I am, through words, actions, or environments, the world always seems to know just how to make me feel like I am an outsider.

To deal with this pain, I spent decades trying to find ways to be a cultural chameleon. I changed my hair. My clothes. My words. I did this to make other people feel more comfortable in the places and spaces we shared. But when I did this—denying my identity in an attempt to fit in—I paid a high price.

Not wanting other people to feel this pain of exclusion, I've spent my entire career working in the social impact space build-ing community and cultures of opportunity, first in the United States and then on a global scale. On paper, I should have been happy. I'd made it. I'd gone from being left on the street as a baby to doing a lot of good in the world. I'd reached a point in my career where I was being asked to give talks at places such as The Guggenheim and the Massachusetts Institute of

Technology. At home, I had an incredible husband who loved me. And sometimes my kids thought that I was actually cool. But no matter the impact I made in the outside world, and no matter how many accolades I received, something was always missing. A deep hole that I could never seem to fill; I still felt like an outsider.

A few years ago, all this hiding and denying caught up with me. I was sitting at my kitchen table in Munich one night reading a study about how the feeling of exclusion shared the same neural pathways as physical pain.[1] I'd read about things like this before, but this was the first time I'd internalized it. It was my awakening. It explained so much of who I was and how I experienced the world. When we feel like an outsider, it hurts. Like *physically* hurts. The in-your-gut, I-wanna-cry kind of pain. A moment of clarity washed over me. This pain I'd been carrying with me, this constant feeling of exclusion wasn't just a feeling—it was an epidemic. I'd been wearing masks and social distancing my entire life. But it was my identity I was masking and cultures I was socially distancing from. I was causing myself so much pain by letting others tell me I didn't belong. I needed to start defining what *belonging* actually was. But not belonging to others. Belonging to myself.

From that moment on, I went all in. I kept a journal, a collection of insights questioning who I am, what I believe in, and what I'm all about. Writing through my thoughts and dissecting my struggles and trauma revealed why I'd lived in physical pain for so long, from not truly knowing my place in the world. These insights explained why I tried to hide parts of my identity and why I allowed strangers to make me angry when they asked me where I was *really* from. I'd been looking for belonging in all the wrong places. I'd allowed the outside world to define *where* and *when* I belonged instead of doing the work on myself, for myself. Most poignantly, I realized I hadn't owned the journey I'd been on. I hadn't seen all the beautiful aspects about myself that made me feel like an outsider as part of my identity that was to be loved.

Although the details and intricacies of my experiences may be different from yours, we all have moments when we feel like an outsider. Moments when we hide or obscure parts of our identity in an attempt to fit in. Maybe it shows up in meeting rooms or job applications. Or maybe it shows up by the way you wear your hair or in how you pronounce your name. We do this because the need to belong is hardwired in all of us. It's part of the human condition. But as we navigate daily life, many of us look to the outside world to feel seen, heard, and valued without first taking the steps to belong to ourselves and understand why we feel like an outsider.

Belonging Begins with You

We're at a moment where diversity, equity, and inclusion (DEI) are no longer topics of the few but widely held expectations for people to thrive in all aspects of life. In a world where so many people still feel like outsiders, belonging is the next critical step in the evolution of DEI. Currently the majority of culture-building programs focus on teams or at organizational levels. They rarely dive deep into the individual identity piece so each of us can define how we want to be seen, heard, and valued on our own terms.

Though well-intentioned, many organizations get these programs wrong. For years, this is what I got wrong. You can't build a culture of belonging *for* people; you have to build a culture of belonging *with* people. To do this, individuals need the space to get to know who they are and define how they want to be seen, heard, and valued on their own terms. Without this foundation, people will continue to wear masks in an attempt to fit in. The roll-over effect of that impacts our culture at home, at work, and in the world. When we mask ourselves, we hide parts of our identity that we need to thrive. And when that happens, we lack safe spaces for each of us to bring forth our authentic selves. The definition of a "safe space" is different for everyone, which makes the individual identity work critical in building a culture of belonging. This is because "culture" is not something people fit into but rather a sum of each of our individual parts.

Like many things that sound obvious, individual identity work is not easy. In a world full of labels, many of us allow our identity to be defined by other people. And the more labels we gather, the more difficult it becomes to untangle the story we tell ourselves about who we are and where we belong. Despite devoting much of my career to creating cultures of belonging and opportunity, this happened to me. I got so caught up in trying to fit in and adapting myself to different cultures that I didn't take the time to truly be a part of those cultures because I wasn't showing up as my authentic self.

You Belong Here—through an exploration of identity and culture—dives into the places this shows up in our lives. This book is for those of us who have walked into a room and felt like we didn't belong, like we have to become "someone else" to feel accepted, and like we have lost ourselves in a world that forces us to hide who we are. It takes us through a journey of personal exploration that allows each of us to **see, claim, edit, and own our identity** so that we can stand firmly when we feel like an outsider and our values are pressure-tested. This critical inner work brings us back to our core, opening ourselves up to which aspects of our identity to leave and which to love. The learnings and frameworks detailed in this book will help us to root ourselves in our authentic identity and define how we want to be seen, heard, and valued on our own terms.

By doing this work, we are rooted in an identity we love, which sets the foundation to create safe spaces at home, at work, and in our community, allowing a culture of belonging to thrive. This book is an ideal companion for those of us who want to create safe spaces for our teams and organizations and understand the critical role belonging plays in building strong cultures within the communities we serve. The Belonging

Journey and accompanying framework are designed to be used as a "step one" with stakeholders. It is an ideal resource for project kickoffs, team cohesion, and culture building as it provides everyone with a shared understanding of who is gathered and how they want to be seen, heard, and valued. The ability to name the parts of each person's identity allows for a greater understanding of the systemic barriers to opportunity for everyone to thrive, while providing a shared language and consistent approach to belonging in workshops and convenings. As we grapple with how to create diverse, equitable, and inclusive cultures, this book provides the necessary foundation to create belonging.

Belonging within Our Four Identities

I would love it if once we found belonging within ourselves, our journey was done. But it's not. Belonging is forever work—a lifelong practice that changes over time. Belonging to ourselves begins by defining and owning our identity, so we have a foundation to root us when we feel like an outsider. Although the systems we live in may deny us that right, understanding that we are all born equal is critical in the journey to belonging. Once we explore what the outsider experience feels like and how belonging is a shared human experience, we go on a Belonging Journey to discover ourselves through an exploration of our four identities that define who we are and how we show up in the world.

OUR FOUR IDENTITIES

Our **Lived Identity** is made up of the aspects of our identity we inherit when we are born.

Our **Learned Identity** includes the parts of our identity that we've chosen or claimed as we make our way through the world.

Our **Lingering Identity** is the identity we default to when we feel like an outsider and fall back into as a survival mechanism.

Our **Loved Identity** is where we find our authentic selves and see ourselves through a lens of empowerment.

As we go on this Belonging Journey, we are going to ask a lot of questions and dig deep into understanding how to see, hear, and value ourselves. This allows us to become the authors of the stories we tell ourselves about who we are and where we belong. To begin, we must revisit our starting point as well as the culture we are born into. When we do this, we are able to fully **see our Lived Identity.** This entails exploring the aspects of our identity that we've inherited at birth such as our race, nationality, sexual orientation, socioeconomic class, and gender as well as examining how these aspects of our identity affect the opportunities in front of us. We will dive into our origin story and question which parts of our Lived Identity we either embrace or hide depending on the room we walk into. The more we feel like an outsider, the more our Lived Identity is amplified. Although we cannot change our starting point, we can change our relationship with these aspects of our identity once they've been identified and we can see where we began.

Next, we will **claim our Learned Identity**. These are the aspects of our identity that we've chosen or claimed as we make our way through the world, including professions, job titles, family, relationships, and education. Here we will define our guiding principles. We will be challenged to think about which of these aspects serve us, which ones don't, and which parts are forced on us by others and the implications this has on the opportunities before us. By claiming our Learned Identity, we can see which systems are set up for equitable access to opportunity and which ones have barriers.

Once we see our Lived Identity and claim our Learned Identity, we take a step back to **edit our Lingering Identity.** This is our default position that is rooted in old stories we tell ourselves about who we are and where we belong. Our Lingering Identity is hardwired into our brain and how we respond because of years of repeating these narratives. It shows up in situations where we feel like an outsider, and we fall back into those old habits as a survival mechanism. This happens to all of us. It happened to me. When the airport taxi driver triggered my Lingering Identity by asking where I was *really* from, I became defensive. I didn't want to answer because I bought into the narrative that the Korean part of me was "less than." When we define this Lingering Identity and understand the cues and triggers that make us feel like an outsider, we can sunset the stories that aren't serving us and rewrite new ones that do.

When we go on this journey to understand our past experiences and how society has established systemic barriers to entry, we can design our own future—a future where we **own our Loved Identity.** Here we view ourselves through a lens of empowerment. We clarify our values. We discover what we are fighting for and who we want fighting beside us. When we fully leverage our Loved Identity and live with authenticity and purpose, we can be seen, heard, and valued in a way that gives us a sense of belonging in any situation. Instead of looking for a seat at someone else's table, we have the tools to build a new one. By going on this Belonging Journey to see, clam, edit, and own our identities, we're able to understand who we are at our core and how we want to show up in the world on our own terms.

The beauty of belonging to yourself is it goes beyond each of us as individuals. When we live with authenticity, we want that for others. Our eyes open to the journey that each of us is on. We see everyone as individuals. Complex. Beautiful. We become curious about their plight because we know what it feels like to be an outsider and experience the pain of exclusion. This realization allows us to see others through a more empathetic lens. We want to ensure the Loved Identity of others is honored in everyday situations. Belonging does not mean we need to be surrounded by others who are just like us. It's about creating safe spaces where opposing viewpoints are seen and heard so we can challenge assumptions and ensure that authentic interactions take place. How do we show up in places where we feel like we don't belong? How do we talk to others with differing perspectives and experiences? How do we set the stage for understanding?

● ● ● ●

I grew into the story I told myself. *I'm too Korean. I'm too female. I'm too opinionated. I'm too radical.* Over time, I became so buried in these stories that weren't serving me that I couldn't recognize where those stories ended and where my real story began. Today, however, when strangers ask, "But where are you *really* from?" I have a response. I tell myself: *You belong here.*

I have found the tools to navigate being an outsider.

I have found my own unique power and beauty in my differences.

I have found my Loved Identity.

My hope is that in the pages that follow you gain the insights and tools to do the same. True belonging is realized when we discover that we are all outsiders, and it's the power of creating spaces for those differences that unites us all.

• 1 •

We Are All Outsiders

For as long as I can remember, I've been a fighter, not a lover. I hated that about myself. And it felt like the world did too. But this didn't happen by accident. Being a fighter was who I was from the day I was born. It was my default position. From being left in a box on the streets of Korea as a baby, to my first memories after I was adopted and transported to a midwestern town in the United States, I was in survival mode. I had a choice: fight, flight, or freeze.

Living in a world where I didn't see myself in anyone, I felt like I didn't fit in anywhere. My parents and neighbors were white. So were my classmates and teachers. I was raised alongside my four sisters. Two were white. One was Korean. And one was from Bangladesh. I wasn't bonded to any of them through genetics. We were like a real-life melting pot. From the moment I woke up in the morning until the time I went to sleep at night, the only person who remotely looked like me on TV was Connie

Chung on the six o'clock evening news. On top of all of this, I had to navigate a culture where being nice was valued above all else. I was taught from an early age to speak only when you were spoken to and never *ever* cause a scene. It was so pervasive in the culture I was raised in that there's even a term for it—"Midwest nice." As a kid, I got used to the silence and watching heads turn when I walked into a room. I got used to people asking me, "Where are you *really* from?" I even got used to people asking me where my *real* parents were. Even though it became less and less surprising, each and every time these microaggressions happened, they hurt.

To this day, I can still feel the pit in my stomach when teachers assigned us the family tree exercise in school, which started with the hospital where we were born, and the anxiety I felt when doctors asked for my family medical history. In both situations I had to respond: "I don't know, I'm adopted." I watched the look in their eyes change from curiosity to pity every time. I wanted to shrink into a corner and cry. I needed to find a way to combat these situations, so I chose to use my voice and fight with my words. But again and again, I was told not to respond, that I had to be *nice*, that nice girls don't fight.

Well, they got that one wrong.

Even though nice girls don't fight, strong ones sure as hell do.

This was my daily experience. I was taught to define myself by what I *was not* instead of what I *was*. When some people looked at me, they saw an Asian kid mired in stereotypes, not the ideas or values I stood for. While others were invited in, I was left on the fringes of places and spaces that were supposedly designed to be shared. I was told I should just be thankful that my parents had saved me from the streets of Korea. That my life was a debt to be paid. That I should be grateful that I got this job. That I should just appreciate that I had a seat at the table. But when you live a life like that, a life of being othered, you need to fight just to be seen. You need to fight harder for your ideas to be heard than someone from within the dominant culture.

As I got older, I realized that my experience wasn't an accident. The world was not designed for someone like me. "Act like us." "Look like us." "Talk like us." "Be nice." "Shrink to make others comfortable." And if I ever found a place where others made me feel like I *did* belong, that in itself would cause an identity crisis. Throughout a difficult adolescence I turned this fight inward. I turned this pent-up angst into self-destruction. During my lowest points, however, the ones who stayed by my side were the outsiders. The ones who struggled with their own pain of exclusion. The ones who had been told they were less than, that their lives were not equal. In their solidarity I began to put the pieces of my life back together. I wouldn't accept how that world fared for me and so many others. I chose to fight.

From Inclusion to Belonging

You may not be able to relate to all of my story, but it's not unique to me and how I experience the world. Maybe you don't live in a different country like Korea, the United States, or Germany. Maybe you don't stand out in your high school yearbook or in family photos. Maybe you don't get asked where you're *really* from. Regardless, we've all experienced times when we've felt like an outsider, moments when we've stepped into a room, felt the silence, and thought to ourselves, *I don't belong here.*

The belonging conversation seems to be taking place everywhere right now. It's happening around kitchen tables, in classrooms, and in boardrooms throughout the world. Belonging is a hot topic because so many people are realizing that having a seat at the table isn't enough. We may have diversity in our workplace, and we may even have programs that give people the opportunity to be included. But despite these advancements, we have to keep pushing as there are still so many people who don't feel that they belong. And if this is the situation we are experiencing, we need to question if we even want a seat at that table, or if it is time for us to build a new one.

To respond to this reckoning, many organizations have made diversity, equity, and inclusion a growing priority in their organizational strategies. The realization that we need to move from inclusion to belonging is finally rising in the workplace. But like anything new, we need to begin by asking different questions: Is our culture designed *for* people or *with* people? Is our culture something we as individuals have to adapt to in order to fit in, or is our culture a sum of each of our individual parts? Who is making the decisions about what our culture is and what it should be?

Creating cultures of belonging has been my forever work since, well, forever. No matter if I was working with teens, adults, artists, nonprofits, or corporations in the United States or globally, all of my jobs since entering the workforce have entailed designing and scaling cultures of belonging and ensuring everyone has equitable access to opportunity. I was asking myself these questions because I knew firsthand what the pain of exclusion feels like. I didn't want others to experience that pain at home, at work, or in the world at large. To build cultures of belonging, many people skip the most important step. For decades, I know I did. I'm still working on it because belonging is a practice, not a destination. To create safe spaces for others, you must first belong to yourself. To discover others, you must first discover yourself and know who you are and how you want to be seen, heard, and valued on your own terms. You need to ask these same questions about your own life and how you show up in the world. This is the key and critical first step to building a culture of belonging—*it starts with you.*

It's in the word itself: *BE—LONG—ING.* BE is to exist, LONG is the desire, and ING is the continual action. Each of us is actively longing to exist. Belonging begins inside each of us as individuals. It begins with you. This desire binds us together. It is a shared human condition. And in every corner of the world, it is this journey that unites us. But when we feel like an outsider and are denied this right by the systems and cultural norms that have been established that work for some but not for all, it hurts. To find and design new ways to be seen, heard, and valued on our own terms, we need to explore what makes us feel like an outsider.

Not Belonging Hurts

Maybe you feel like an outsider at home. You feel out of place at a family dinner, or when your teenage kids tell you how uncool you are. Or maybe it happens in your community. You walk into a store, restaurant, or your neighborhood block party and immediately feel like you don't fit in. Or maybe these feelings arise when you're at school or at work. You enter your new classroom on your first day to a sea of unfamiliar faces, or you start a new job and you're introduced to a new community of coworkers.

Your heartbeat spikes. You feel the quiet, cold stares. You feel the eyes looking you up and down like a virtual body scan. All of us experience this feeling at some point in our lives. When I ask people to tell me about a time they felt like they didn't belong, they usually point to an everyday experience. Their responses start with "I was at work and I had to go to this meeting" or "I was forced to go to this party." They all end the same: "I felt like there was a giant spotlight on me." This feeling had little to do with their career, their role, or their stage in life and instead was simply a human response that has been baked in for millennia. These moments that shape our sense of belonging are hardwired in each of us, and many of us have to navigate these experiences on a daily basis. As an example, let's take a look at my average workday:

- I wake up (me).

- Get the kids to school (family).

- Commute on the Ubahn, the metro in Munich, Germany, where I currently live (world).

- Go to work (workplace).

- Go to dinner (community).

- Come home (family).

- Go to sleep (me).

- Repeat.

On any given day, throughout each of these locations and situations, I am weaving in and out of feelings of *inclusion* to those of *exclusion*. I am always prepared for the worst while hoping for the best. Because of this uncertainty, my brain and body are constantly on high alert, and these sensations and thoughts could change even within the walls of these experiences.

As I go from meeting to meeting, depending on the participants, shifts take place. In the mornings, for instance, I'm usually the lone American in rooms full of Europeans. When the United States wakes up and I head into virtual meetings, I'm the European in a screen full of Americans. In both situations I feel like the outsider. And this doesn't stop with the country's culture, as every meeting room is different. Some days, I am leading a meeting and sometimes I am a participant. Some days, I am the dissenting opinion and other times I am giving virtual high fives. This continues on my train ride home based on who shows up at the same time I do. Maybe it's as simple as walking onto the platform and getting a warm smile from a toddler in a stroller. Other days, it is me shielding my daughter from a stranger yelling at us to get out of "their" country. Yes, this happens more often than I care to remember, no matter where I am in the world. It's a roll of the dice.

During each of these moments, the brain categorizes the environment to determine if it's safe or a threat. This response is part of our DNA, one of our oldest survival mechanisms. When this happens, our fight-or-flight response kicks in. We tense up. Our brains are telling us to run because there is a real and present danger. If it turns out that the perceived environment is safe, we start to calm down. Our heartbeat stabilizes. Things begin to normalize within our bodies. Our shoulders drop. The threat is over. But even so, the experience and pain that comes with it becomes hardwired in us because we never want to be in that situation again. As much as we might try to avoid these moments, they will always be a part of our lives. Feeling like an outsider is an ongoing human experience. And when it happens to us, it doesn't feel good.

Researchers Geoff MacDonald and Mark Leary published a study in *Psychological Bulletin* that demonstrates how the feelings of exclusion share the same neural pathways as pain.[2] It feels like actual, physical pain. If you've experienced this, you aren't alone. It's a normal response. It hurts. Often you can feel it before you can name it, because our bodies have been hardwired to tell us this too is dangerous. We go on high alert. Our brain signals that the situation needs immediate attention. This wiring of the physical pain and not feeling a sense of belonging is a danger sign. And we will do anything to avoid this state and not experience that pain again.[3]

When this happens, we are rooted squarely in survival mode. In response to not wanting to go through the internal panic and experience the pain from exclusion, over time we begin to make changes in an attempt to adapt to our surroundings instead of standing firmly in our Loved Identity. We start changing our hair. We choose different clothes. We change the words we use. Some of us even change our names. But in service of what? We push this pain from that moment down deep into our everyday life. It lingers and festers and grows. And that pain becomes loneliness, sadness, and despair. It turns from a warning into a disease.[4] With so many people experiencing this cycle in their lives, a lack of belonging isn't just a feeling—it's an epidemic.

Dr. Arline Geronimus defines this prolonged effect of being othered with the term "weathering." In her book *Weathering: The Extraordinary Stress of Ordinary Life on the Body in an Unjust Society*, she shares research gathered from her forty-year career in the public health sector, wrestling with racial and class injustice. Geronimus's findings demonstrate how being othered and the accompanying stress that comes with it can not only wear us down mentally and emotionally but physically as well. The impact that weathering has on our bodies lowers our defenses, which in turn increases the rate at which we age. In short, othering is a killer. According to Geronimus:

> Weathering afflicts human bodies—all the way down to the cellular level—as they grow, develop, and age in a systemically and historically racist, classist, stigmatizing, or xenophobic society. Weathering damages the cardiovascular, neuroendocrine, immune, and metabolic body systems in ways that leave people vulnerable to dying far too young, whether from infectious diseases like COVID-19, or the early onset and pernicious progression of chronic diseases like hypertension. Because of the physiological impacts of unrelenting exposure to stressors in one's physical and social environment, as well as the high physiological effort that coping with chronic stressors entails, weathering means that relatively young people in oppressed groups can be biologically old.[5]

The Dangerous "Algorithm of Sameness"

To remedy these feelings of exclusion, many of us look to the outside world to define our sense of belonging and fulfill this fundamental human need. We constantly search for proof points of belonging in our daily lives and allow others to define who we are and determine how we are seen, heard, and valued. To find belonging, we look for people that look like us, gravitating toward them as friends and coworkers. We look for social cues of acceptance, and we stay there. We look for moments of affirmation from others, and we go back for more. It is through that social proof of others that we get the feeling of safety. *These are my people,* we say to ourselves. *They get me. This is totally normal.*

As if navigating our daily lives wasn't already complex, we now live in a world where social media hasn't just made this possible, it has made this *probable* as it's curated for extreme sameness. Social media tells us the things we should buy based on our previous shopping history. It tells us the things we should listen to based on our last song. It presents news based on our search history. All of this becomes an illusion of comfort. That people see us. That the world is like us. But sameness is not equity. This algorithm of sameness is dangerous, and we are all paying the price.

These seismic shifts toward sameness are embedded in our interactions with the digital *and* the physical world. The algorithms identify what we consume and our perception of how the world is and is not. As these small nudges toward sameness compound, when opposing viewpoints, thoughts, ideas, or concepts go against this tsunami of reinforcing information, it feels like we are an outsider. All of the data and information going in seems to be saying that this is the norm. And the norm has been built on systems that work for some but not for all.

Our culture is also an algorithm. It is full of patterns and social cues that work like a predictable system that is reinforced by repeated choices. For example, here in Munich jaywalking is rarely seen, but not for the reasons I thought. I had assumed it was because Germany is such a "rules-based" culture. But what I learned is it's really about modeling safe behavior for children, and they take that collective responsibility very seriously. I always tell visitors to be aware of jaywalking to avoid strangers screaming "child killers" at them when crossing the road.

When we think about our personal interactions, we do the same thing with the choices that we make. A few years ago, a woman invited me to speak about leadership to a group of executives. Before the speech, she pulled me aside and shared that she was struggling to find her identity at work. Like a lot of people, she told me she was suffering from imposter syndrome: a feeling like even though she had the job, she wasn't qualified to have a seat at the table.[6] She said she didn't fit into the business world and that she wasn't "professional" enough. I asked her to focus on the word "professional" and interrogate what it really means. After a long pause, she told me she'd never actually questioned that before. We examined how the term "professional" is viewed differently all around the world and how it changes from company to company and from border to border.

For some, "professional" means wearing a neatly pressed suit, not displaying emotions, and using formal language. For others, it means donning a black T-shirt and Vans, speaking in soundbites, and communicating through memes. "We need to define which aspects of 'professional' are meaningful to you," I told her, "the aspects that bring out your own unique talents so that you can thrive." A few months after that event, she told me how much of a difference that shift had made for her. Rather than trying to mold or shape-shift to the environment around her, she took a new job and now brings her full self to work, which has created space for others to do the same. Her new-found confidence may not be typical or the same as the other people around her, but it has worth, and it matters.

Although we may feel alone when experiencing these feelings, this woman's circumstance is far from unique. So often, organizations within their own hiring strategies ask themselves if candidates are a "culture fit," meaning they would fit in with the existing culture, or a "culture add," meaning someone who will bring different ideas, perspectives, and experiences to the team. While "culture fit" could accelerate the algorithm of sameness, "culture add" though well-intentioned often puts people in harm's way. They are often made to feel responsible for transforming the workplace, which can be lonely work when the nature of their role is rooted in pushing boundaries and establishing new ways of doing things within an existing work-place culture.

Social entrepreneur Maggie De Pree wanted to find a new way forward. For years she felt like she couldn't bring her full self to the workplace. After hearing so many people inside organizations reinforce the narrative they didn't feel professional enough, she cofounded in 2012 the League of Intrapreneurs. This community provides support for individuals who have been brought into organizations to push forward the most important initiatives of our time around people and the planet. Today the League of Intrapreneurs is comprised of more than twenty thousand changemakers who have committed to doing this courageous and necessary work. "We devalue transformational care-driven roles that are the future of work in favor of transactional work," she told me in an interview.[7] It takes courage to enter rooms knowing full well that people will roll their eyes when these changemakers and culture shifters voice their "wild ideas," Maggie added. They are often considered "misfits" or "weirdos," and this courage is under-recognized and severely underappreciated. She wanted to create a safe space where individuals could come as they are to recharge and share ideas and experiences to continue to have the energy to do this work.

Whether we realize it, over time the experiences of people not fully seeing our strengths, valuing our contributions, or allowing our voices to be heard shape the stories we tell ourselves about our own worth. In this way we give away our power. But

A DAY IN YOUR LIFE

Describe an average day in your life. Imagine what you do from the moment you wake up until you go to sleep. Visualize the environments where those things happen.

- Where do you feel included?

- Where do you feel like an outsider?

- What are the social cues that make you feel that way?

This is a way to see opportunities for action within your various environments to explore deeper when you feel like an outsider.

our power is rooted in our own identity as *we* define it. When others strip it from our core, the choices we have in life change. This is why we all need to ask the hard questions. If we don't, we are unintentionally putting our sense of belonging into the hands of others and we end up giving away our power.

• 2 •

Belong to Yourself

It wasn't only in my personal life where I fought to be seen and for my voice to be heard. I made a professional career of fighting. Not in that "get in the ring, put on your gloves, and box" kind of fighting. I fought for various causes: the arts, education, and equity in nonprofit organizations. Because of the nature of the work, it was grounded in a clear purpose, and everyone involved was fighting for the same things. Whether I was an intern or an executive director, the work was always about making the world a better place. And it was clear who the "us" was. We were the ones fighting injustice. We were the ones making a difference. And everyone else who wasn't doing this work was part of the problem. It was the government. It was corporations. It was "them." It was clear which side I was on, and people were either with us or against us. But were they?

When we start to pull on a thread of an issue, it often becomes tangled pretty fast. We like neat and tidy answers to
complex problems. I used to lead a nonprofit organization in
the United States whose mission was to provide a culture of opportunity for people to make social and economic progress in
their lives and communities. Every day we welcomed students
from under-resourced communities into our spaces and classrooms for creative exploration and career training. So many
people outside of the organization would say if the students
just "tried harder" in school, they would be successful. If their
parents were more involved, they would get better grades. If
they would just "pull themselves up by their bootstraps," they
could get a job. These statements sent me into a rage. I saw
the barriers our brilliant students faced. When you are working
two minimum-wage jobs where time off to attend your child's
parent-teacher conference isn't an option, you learn pretty fast
that presence is a privilege.

A Brookings Institute study highlights the foundational issue
of these outcomes: lack of access to resources such as skilled
teachers and quality curriculum. The disparity of opportunity
makes the American educational system one of the most inequitable in the industrialized world.[8] This lack of academic support
was just one of the mountains of barriers our students faced
before they even got their "boots" on each morning. If you grew
up in this environment, you would see the face of real innovation. On a daily basis our students had to hack every system they

encountered. The lived experiences that they showed us every single day couldn't be taught in business school. Their agility in navigating difficult situations and their resilience in the face of oppression were at levels that would crush the most senior leaders in many organizations. So, no, please don't talk to me about "bootstraps" and the importance of "trying just a little bit harder."

Through my fight for equity, the further I got into the work, the less patience I had because with every moment that passed, someone else had lost an opportunity. It was easy for me to make other people the "them," because so many people had not truly seen the brilliance of the students despite the systems of oppression they faced. But as the anger became embedded deeper and deeper within me, I began to use the same narratives to marginalize "them" in the same way that they were marginalizing the students. If anything was going to change, however, it was going to take all of us to get to the other side of these issues. But instead of building bridges, I burned them. Rather than calling people in, I called people out. It was my superpower. I too was dividing the world into an us-versus-them culture. I realized that *how* I was using my fight needed to change.

The Illusion of Us versus Them

We live in a time when extreme polarization is the norm. We see it in the news and in politics. We see it in our meetings and at holiday dinners. We are having tough conversations, or maybe we chose to avoid them altogether. Instead of listening to understand, we listen to defend as we go further and further into our corners. Due to the reinforcing flood of information through our personalized algorithms of incoming information that tells us we are right, we plant ourselves firmer within the positions we hold. In turn, this deepens the biases we hold in our lives. Our brains shortcut critical thinking by telling ourselves that we are right, even if the facts we hold are only part of the story. The part of the story we want to believe. The part of the story we have lived.

But this isn't confined to conversations around politics over holiday dinners. This process happens every day. When we walk into work and we don't see others that look like us or people that have our same lived and learned experiences, bias kicks in, and it works both ways. The brain does that same auto-categorization toward sameness. It fills in the blanks with stories about those around the table based on the tsunami of information that has been curated for us throughout our lifetime. And those blanks could be filled with stories that are blatantly false. When this happens, we have firmly planted ourselves in the us narrative and forced others to become the them. We have not actually invested the time to understand their experience and why they believe what they believe and act in the manner in which they act. We project the same feelings we had been trying to avoid for ourselves onto others.

When we don't address bias head on, this not only creates a toxic culture, it also causes real harm. It has a cascading effect for everyone. People stop speaking up. They stop showing up. And often, the people that are most impacted by this bias are unfairly tasked with the responsibility of educating and designing the way out. This is why building safe spaces is critical for cultures of belonging to thrive. But who is defining who's out and who's in? Who holds the power in these situations?

When people without diverse lived and learned experiences are making decisions for the culture that is being created, bias masks the pain points within these environments and people retreat into us-versus-them behavior. Only representation by people with these experiences can combat that because they know the challenges firsthand. I struggled with this when I made the choice to join a global corporation after spending years in the nonprofit sector. I thought I was being given a chance to use business as a force for good. That I would have the opportunity to transform systems from the inside out so that we could build new systems that work for everyone. But as I reached out to nonprofits wanting to forge partnerships, they looked at me with that same glare of mistrust that I gave when I myself worked in that sector. I was now the them.

But what if there is not an us or a them? What if we are all just trying to belong? What if we could see and honor each other's humanity?

The Search for Belonging

A few years back, I was introduced to Daniel Wordsworth, a social innovator who went on a journey to discover what ties us together as humans. Daniel has worked with people that were being displaced in some of the world's most extreme situations of conflict. He was in Darfur, El Salvador, and the Congo. He has dedicated his life to creating opportunity for people in some of the most challenging environments of our time. His job is to ensure that millions of people can find a way forward in unimaginable situations.

For those who have not experienced this type of trauma, you cannot imagine the world in which Daniel and those inside refugee camps live. The average stay inside a refugee camp is not six days or twelve weeks. According to the Brookings Institution, displacement is between ten and twenty-six years! More than a decade.[9] People are spending a generation in a community that is labeled as "temporary." One of the camps that Daniel worked in consisted of twelve sectors, and in the geographic area of his sector alone, it took four hours to drive from one end of that community to the other. This wasn't a camp—*it was a metropolis.* People told him to just give the refugees supplies for their "basic needs." To keep his objectivity. To not get close to them. To not get to know refugees' names. To not celebrate their birthdays. To not become a part of their lives.

But Daniel did not accept this. While sitting with him in a quiet lodge in Montana during a convening of thought leaders, I asked, "How do you do it? How do you keep hope in a world where you see suffering like that?" Daniel's response will stay with me for the rest of my life. He shared his own search for meaning by trying to find what makes us human, the connection we all have. He went on a two-year journey to discover the thing that binds us all together. He talked to priests and community leaders. Mothers and friends. And what he found reframed my beliefs about humanity.

With quiet intensity, Daniel told me that we need to believe that every human is a thing of great wonder. That we are all born with a gift, and the act of finding that gift and sharing it with the world makes us all human. This is the journey. That is our right. The greatest realization a person can have is the realization of their own worth. We can only realize that when we share our gifts with others freely. But when society and power are in play, they will make people hide or stamp out that gift so they can't give it to others. This is when human suffering begins. Daniel explained how the world is an abundant, beautiful place. People are overwhelmingly good and they are desperate for the opportunity to be good and do good. "There is a place for everyone," he told me. "It is our work to unleash that abundance to all the places of scarcity that exist."[10] Daniel worked on this every day.

Just by being born into this world, we are worthy of love and belonging. But there are so many barriers to people loving their identity. Through policies and practices, many of us are denied the realization of our full potential. The policies tell us we are not valued as equal to those with power and privilege in today's systems. They strip us of our identity and rob us of the opportunity to belong as we are and as we want to be. They make our journey toward wholeness seem like an impossible road.

The aftermath of a system where people are not seen, heard, or valued has lasting effects on both the individual and the collective. When we examine our assumptions of who we are and how we fit in the world, we see it more clearly. So many systems aren't bent or misaligned—they're flat-out broken. We see entire cultures being oppressed for generations because of the actions and decisions of those in positions of power. And when you are an outsider in those cultures, you pay the highest price. When the dominant culture says, "dress this way and you can be one of us," "talk this way," "your name is too difficult to pronounce," "you are not professional enough," you may change your identity to make it easier for others. This results in simultaneously losing yourself along the way. The parts we should see as beautiful, we start to view as aspects of ourselves that are less than.

In the early 2000s, during the fight for marriage equality in the United States, many of my friends and colleagues shared with me their pain of not being seen, heard, and valued. "You know you are equal. You are worthy," I told them. "The rights granted to you are not equal, but you my friend are perfect, just as you are. So together we fight. We fight to reclaim what is rightfully yours. Equity." But what would it take to tip the world from exclusion—one of us versus them—to one of inclusion?

One of belonging? Systems are made up of people. And policies are written by people. And people want to belong. At the end of the day, there is only *you*. Belonging begins when we realize we are all born worthy of being seen, heard, and valued on our own terms.

From We to Me

The conversation I had with Daniel unleashed what felt like decades of frustration around the issues I had been fighting for. It became clear that the person at the epicenter of my suffering was myself. I was grappling with my own humanity, and even though I could clearly see the us and the them, I hadn't seen the *me*.

"I think your nerves are raw," Daniel said to me. "You need to speak to yourself with kindness. You wouldn't say those same things to a friend that you are saying about yourself." He saw me. I was exhausted. I was tired of fighting. My whole life I'd allowed others to define my identity, like so many of us do, and it was time to heal that pain. To do that, I had to reclaim my own narrative about my worth so I could begin to fully love my identity. Before I could work on the *we* of community or organizations, I needed to focus on the *me*—that's where the work began. The stories we tell ourselves, however, are not easy to edit. Our neural pathways are like muscle memory, hardwired in our belief systems. These repeating experiences we have over our lifetime write the story that we tell ourselves about who we are. If the foundation is faulty or miswired, it becomes more difficult to unwire and rewire as we get older.[11] We have to unlearn how we process these signals rooted in trauma and rewire them toward empathy and understanding.

My career in the corporate world began leading learning programs throughout Europe, the Middle East, and Africa. I had seen firsthand the power of inclusive environments that shaped equitable outcomes for students, and I knew I wanted to work on this issue throughout the world. I spent years researching how we learn and the levers we can use within our systems for better outcomes for students. So much of my focus was rooted in the neuroscience of *how we learn* versus *what we learn* and understanding how we process information and the conditions that help us develop the ability to thrive. We can see how critical support, care, and love is in our development and how a lack of belonging shapes our bodies and brains. So how are we processing that information, and what are the conditions that help us use it as a force for good? When it comes to belonging, understanding the foundation of our beliefs, how we learn, and how we remember things is critical.

Despite the human brain being incredibly complex, the basics of how we learn are quite simple. During our lifetime we're constructing knowledge like building blocks. The environments and experiences we're exposed to and go through early on play a starring role in shaping our advancement over a lifetime. A strong foundation leads to the ability to stack learning and mental models on top of each other, whereas the opposite makes this difficult. The environment we are exposed to is not only important; it is crucial to learning. Neuroscientists use the term "productive tension" to describe the role of pushing our brains to learn at a specific point in time.[12] Some stress is good to help push us to stretch and grasp new concepts and ideas. It builds new neural pathways. But too much stress shuts us down and learning can't happen.

Everyone has that point when learning something new. The frustration that you can't get it as you try and test new ways, then that fabulous moment when it clicks and you feel amazing. You got it. You learned something. But if you don't know where your next meal will come from or where you will sleep at the end of the day, your brain can't focus on the square root of 144. It would be processing too much stress. It triggers that reptilian brain that stems from thousands of years of evolution when we go into fight, flight, freeze, or fawn mode, which stops learning in its tracks and inhibits us from making sound, well-thought-out, and informed decisions.[13]

If the foundation is set in an unhealthy way during our critical developmental years, it becomes not only more difficult to rewire those pathways, but it serves as the primary building block on which all other experiences build. All these experiences—whether good or bad, supportive or unsupportive—pile up, and the older we get, the more our behavior repeats based on those experiences. If our initial experiences were those of individualism and control, our behaviors were shaped to learn and respond through those modes. If those early experiences were full of collaboration and coaching, those are the behaviors that show up later in our work and personal lives. But imagine if your brain is stuck in that mode from a lifetime of experiences where you feel you are in danger. Imagine if you always felt like an outsider. It's only logical these responses to everything would become hardwired.

So, yes, when speaking to Daniel, my nerves had become raw. I was tired from fighting. Not just in support of the causes that I advocate for. I was tired from a lifetime of people telling me I didn't belong. It was time to break out of this cycle and understand the journey I'd been on to define how I wanted to belong to myself on my own terms. The desire to belong to ourselves on our own terms resonates universally, no matter the background of people I've interviewed throughout the world as well as in countless conversations in my personal life. When people learn I'm a belonging researcher, they open up and share with me their own stories of exclusion, expressing a longing to live with authenticity and to feel like they belong.

In order for each of us to learn how to belong to ourselves, we need to go on a journey. To question everything. To dig deep. To reexamine parts of our identity we haven't acknowledged. To bring into the light the pieces of us that we have hidden over time from others. This is the journey to belonging. To let down our hair. To say our name confidently. To reclaim our identity.

DEFINE YOUR US AND THEM

Reflect back on a time when you were engaging in an us-versus-them moment in your life.

- Who was the us in the story and why?

- Who was the them in the story and why?

- What was the topic of debate that put you in this us-versus-them mind-set?

Now swap roles and describe this interaction as the us *and* as the them.

- What could you do to ensure that you see a fuller picture of the them in this situation?

- What are ways that you can *call people in* versus *calling people out* in that interaction?

When we pause to leverage empathy to fully see the context that people are bringing to a conversation, we can better engage in civil discourse and honor each other's humanity, even when we don't agree.

• 3 •

Your Four Identities

For many of us the systemic barriers to living authentically—rooted in an identity we love—are so high and so steep that we skip the exploration of what the barriers are and why they exist. We accept the systems as truth and believe that this is the way things need to be.

- "This is what a family looks like."

- "This is what a community values."

- "This is how I should dress at work."

- "This is what 'professional' is."

- "These are the things I should value."

We let others tell us we don't belong, even if it isn't with their words, it is through their policies and actions. We are surrounded by situations that tell us that story over and over in our

OUR FOUR IDENTITIES

Each of us has four identities that play a critical role in who we are and how we show up in the world.

- Our **Lived Identity** is made up of the aspects of our identity we inherit when we are born.

- Our **Learned Identity** includes the parts of our identity that we've chosen or claimed as we make our way through the world.

- Our **Lingering Identity** is the identity we default to when we feel like an outsider and fall back into as a survival mechanism.

- Our **Loved Identity** is where we show up as our authentic selves and see ourselves through a lens of empowerment.

lives. But it doesn't have to be this way. We need to question why things are the way they are. We need to examine what choices have been made for us, and which choices we are able to make for ourselves.

It is time to define how we want to be seen, heard, and valued on our own terms. It is time we design and build a new table where we all belong. It is time to fight. And this fight for belonging starts with you.

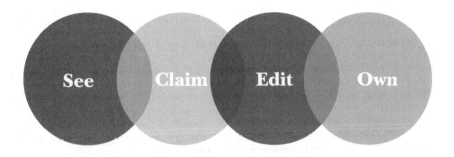

EXHIBIT 1. The Belonging Journey

Source: Kim Dabbs

• • • •

The Belonging Journey

When we go on this Belonging Journey (see exhibit 1), we discover and define our four identities to live in an identity we love. When you reconcile your Lived, Learned, and Lingering Identities with the aspiration of being seen, heard, and valued on your own terms, you can live authentically in your Loved Identity. This means that you see the aspects of your identity that you've inherited and the world you are born into, you've claimed your choices, and you've edited the stories you have told yourself about who you are and where you belong. When you can do this, you own your Loved Identity and can stand firm in any situation.

See our Lived Identity. To see the aspects of our identity that we inherit, we need to understand the cultures and systems we are born into that make us feel like an outsider. Although we cannot change our starting point, we can change our relationship with these aspects of our identity once they've been identified and we can see where we began.

Claim our Learned Identity. To claim our identity and not let others define it for us, we need to question the stories we've been told about who we are and where we belong. By doing so, we can challenge the norms that we live with and establish our guiding principles as they help us to claim the parts of our identity that serve us and discard those that don't.

Edit our Lingering Identity. We need to edit our default position that we fall back into as a survival mechanism when we feel like we are an outsider. We will no longer accept environments where we feel forced to hide aspects of our identity and can challenge the systems that place judgment on our right to belong.

Own our Loved Identity. To belong to ourselves, we need to show up authentically and see ourselves through a lens of empowerment. We accomplish this by transforming our Lived, Learned, and Lingering Identities into one we love.

● ● ● ●

The first step in this journey to belonging is to **see our Lived Identity.** These are the aspects we've inherited like race, nationality, ethnicity, sexual orientation, socioeconomic class, and gender. We dive into our origin story and question which parts of our Lived Identity we either step into or hide depending on the room we walk into.[14] By doing so, we gain clarity on the world we are born into and the systems and conditions that shaped our developmental years.

Next, we **claim our Learned Identity.** These are the aspects of our identity that we've chosen or claimed, including professions, job titles, family, relationships, and education. We define our guiding principles to determine how we want to be seen, heard, and valued. We will be challenged to think about which of these aspects serve us, which ones don't, and which parts are forced upon us by others and the implications this has on the opportunities before us. This allows us to identify which systems are set up for equitable access to opportunity and which ones have barriers.

The third step in our Belonging Journey is where we **edit our Lingering Identity.** This is our default position that's rooted in old stories we tell ourselves about who we are and what we deserve. It's hardwired into our brain and how we respond. It shows up in situations where we feel like an outsider, and we fall back into those old habits as a survival mechanism. It happens to all of us. When we define this identity and understand the cues and triggers that make us feel like an outsider, we can sunset the stories that aren't serving us and rewrite new ones that do.

REFLECT ON YOUR IDENTITY

Reflect on your identity and how you describe it.

- Does this description change between formal and informal settings?

- Are there circumstances where you consistently show up as your full self?

Hold that with you as we go through this journey to see, claim, edit, and own your identity.

When we go on this journey to understand our past experiences and how society has established barriers to entry, we can design our own future—a future where we **own our Loved Identity.** It is at this fourth step that we view ourselves as we are and as we want to be. And we do this through a lens of empowerment. We clarify our values. We sunset the stories that aren't serving us and step into the ones that do. We define how we want to be seen, heard, and valued. We discover what we are fighting for and who we want fighting beside us. When we fully leverage our Loved Identity and live with authenticity and purpose, we can be seen, heard, and valued in a way that gives us a sense of belonging in any situation. Instead of looking for a seat at someone else's table, we have the tools to build a new one.

Through this process of defining our identity and understanding how to be seen, heard, and valued on our own terms, our eyes open to the journey of others. We become curious about their plight as we know what it feels like to be an outsider and experience the pain of exclusion. This realization allows us to see others through a more empathetic lens. We can use this power to ensure the lived, learned, and loved experiences of ourselves, and others are honored in everyday situations. As we go through this exploration of our Lived, Learned, and Lingering Identities, we are going to embrace the identity we love. This is the gift we are giving to ourselves and sharing with the world.

Now it is your time. Your time to be seen, heard, and valued on your own terms. To name your gift. To find your power. Because when you find your power, you can change the world.

• 4 •

Lived Identity

The identity we inherit.
The parts of us we are born with
and the culture we are born into.

I've never really known how my life began. As a kid, I called Michigan home. When I introduced myself, I would say, "I am American." That's who I was and that is the identity I claimed. But as I got older, it dawned on me that I was leaving out the most important part: it really isn't how my story started. I inherited two identities. One, my Korean side. One, my American side. The problem was that both identities were complex, and both made me feel like an outsider. I grew up in a culture where white was the default, male was the dominant, and American was the dream.

That's all I knew. That's all I saw. That was the culture I inherited, and everywhere I turned, proof points for these beliefs showed up in words, policies, and social cues. This created a

lifelong feeling of "less than" for me. This first building block
was the foundation of my identity. This made the creation of my
origin story excruciating because I was neither the default, the
dominant, nor the dream. I felt like an outsider, defined by the
things I *wasn't*, not the things I *was*. "You're not white." "You're
not Korean." "You're not American." "You're not rich." "You're
not male." The more these experiences stacked, the more I hid
parts of my Lived Identity. The parts that I inherited. The parts
that made me, me.

But what was I supposed to do? As an outsider, in order to
fit in, I felt I had to keep myself small and hide the parts of my
identity I was gifted at birth to be nice. There was no roadmap
for that. So rather than claiming the Korean part of my identity,
I pretended it didn't exist. I hid it.

See Your Lived Identity

The Belonging Journey begins with knowing your origin story.
It serves as the foundation of your Lived Identity—all the aspects of ourselves that we've inherited such as our name, race,
nationality, ethnicity, gender, socioeconomic class, physical and
mental abilities, and sexual orientation. We all have an origin
story because we all came from *someone* and *somewhere*. It's one
of the most fundamental things that we share, across time and
borders.

You may be thinking, "Of course, I know my race, gender, and
nationality." Your Lived Identity, however, isn't just a one-word

answer, it's an exploration. To truly understand your starting point, look at the culture you were born into and how that affects the opportunities in front of you. Take a moment to better see which aspects you hide or mask. This is necessary foundational work so you can proudly see, hear, and value yourself on your own terms. Whether we realize it or not, we all deny ourselves parts of our Lived Identity. For me, it was my Asian-ness. I didn't see it as part of who I am. So many interactions around that side of my identity from others had been dehumanizing, which stopped me from fully embracing it. For so long, I didn't consider my Asian-ness as a part of my identity that should be loved.

Maybe for you, it's similar. You reject your race, nationality, or ethnicity. Or maybe it shows up in the ways you hide your gender, socioeconomic class, or sexual orientation. To understand those formative narratives and the stories we tell ourselves about our lived experiences, we need to first see them and begin to change our relationship with them. When we do this, we reframe the aspects of our Lived Identity that we have habitually hidden as the things that make us powerful.

Sound easy? I wish it were. The path to get there is hard and that's not by our own design. The us-versus-them culture in the world is a force. Many of us have not looked through the lens of how we were brought into the world and the culture and circumstances that surrounded us. Instead, we have accepted the narratives that others have told us about ourselves as truth.

We hide our name, our language, or our accent to blend in, to make the places we share more comfortable for others. But when we hide who we are, we deny ourselves a future of showing up as our authentic selves and growing into the person we want to become. These aspects of our identity are carried forward in our lives, at work, and at home.

When feeling like an outsider is a daily experience, we avoid the pain of not belonging by obscuring these things we have been born with because of the culture of sameness that surrounds us. A friend of mine changed his name and perfected his English accent because he worked in a call center in Mexico that served customers in the United States. He felt dismissed if people heard a hint of his Lived Identity through his voice. He's not alone. Hiding our accents and changing our names on résumés is common practice. And the research shows why people do it. A study by Society for Human Resource Management (SHRM), the leading global human resource organization, showed "applicants with white-sounding names were 50 percent more likely to be contacted for interviews than those with typical black names."[15]

We may not think about it very much, but this also shows up in the food of our culture. When I interviewed a woman who was raised by first-generation immigrant Asian parents in the United States, she shared that the lunch her family prepared became one of those lunchtime table traumatic things in school. Her food wasn't packed in Ziplock bags and brown paper sacks like so many of her friends. Her lunch looked different and it smelled different. When seeing the food her family had prepared for her, like dumplings and chicken feet, the kids at the lunchroom table would tease her, laughing while asking "You actually eat that?" The pain of exclusion that came with these responses stayed with her throughout her life. This lived experience highlighted the difference in that moment that made her want to hide who she was and where she came from. Rather than seeing the food of her culture as a thing of beauty, she felt embarrassment, which carried into how she saw her own Lived Identity.

How far do you carry these types of experiences forward into your life? At work? At home? We need to make space for that so we can see our Lived Identities. In order to do that, however, we must first see our starting point and the culture we were born into.

The Other

Yodit Mesfin Johnson saw her Lived Identity from the day she was born. She was raised to see that she had just as much right as anyone to make her voice heard. The daughter of a Detroit public school teacher and community organizer, Yodit recalled an early life lesson to take up space and to challenge the assumptions about where she belonged. Generations of women in her family had passed down this belief. Yodit's maternal grandmother had helped gender diversify Sears Roebuck Company,

her great-grandmother had been one of the first Black women
to work in the Syracuse China Factory, and her dad's mother
had been the first woman elected to parliament in Ethiopia.
Because of the country's political unrest in the 1960s, Yodit's
grandmother used what resources she could to get Yodit's dad
to the United States. He met Yodit's mom in college, where he
surrounded himself with intellectuals and professors and raised
awareness of what was happening in his home country.

Yodit hailed from a family of strong women who saw their
Lived Identity and learned how to make their voices heard.
And the space they took up made space for generations to
come. But even though this deeply seated belief was rooted
in the fact each and every one of us are born equal, the culture she experienced made Yodit feel like she was the other.
Being othered, which founder John Powell of the Othering and
Belonging Institute at UC Berkeley described as "any practice
that denies someone's humanity," was Yodit's baseline. "I have
the language for it now," she told me, "as I've been doing this
work for a long time. But when I was navigating life in my formative years, it wasn't (just) overt acts of racism or sexism. For
me, othering was an embodiment. When I walk into a place and
everything from the people to the sounds, smells, and even the
colors and the way the furniture is laid out makes me keenly
aware it was not made with me in mind, I can just feel it."[16] And
that feeling isn't just a feeling that passes once the experience
is over. It takes a toll.

Yodit's experience has led to a lifetime of being able to see her Lived Identity. She has leveraged this power to fight inequitable systems. She doesn't know any other way. She told me she's a "recovering reformist" as she learned through her experiences that these systems are working as they were designed to. They were designed for exclusion. They were designed for unequal outcomes. They were designed to deny people's humanity. Because of that, Yodit isn't looking to reform these systems, she's working to radically reimagine futures outside of those systems. The power of seeing not only changes your relationship to who you are, it opens the door to opportunity for generations. This begins with seeing the aspects of our identity that we inherited at birth as well as seeing the systems that we were born into that have included or excluded parts of us.

The parts that make us equal.

The parts that make us worthy.

The parts that make us human.

Hide and Seek

I haven't always seen my Lived Identity. My formative experiences were radically different from Yodit's, but the daily feelings of othering were exactly the same. Growing up, when I introduced myself, I tried really hard to insist I was American, that I wasn't Korean. But the truth was, I *was* Korean. It was part of my identity that I couldn't run away from, no matter how hard I tried. The more I attempted to suppress my Asian-ness, to take attention away from it, the more attention it was given. And to change this, I needed to understand why I was hiding the fact I was Korean. The world told me it was something that was less than, and it did a good job of almost convincing me that was true.

For the first decade of my life, when I introduced my origin story, it began: "I arrived in the United States in the winter to begin my life with my family...." My origin story started as an American. My arrival date was so prominent that my adopted family called it my Homecoming Day—a day we celebrate every year just like celebrating birthdays and anniversaries. It was an important day for me, but this wasn't because of the adoption. It was important because it was the only solid data point about my life I had until then. Because I was abandoned as a baby, my birthday was assigned to me by the adoption agency. Who knew if I was an Aquarius or a Pisces? But my Homecoming Day? That date, I knew for sure. That date was mine.

I still don't know what happened in the first months of my life. Nor do I know if I was loved or lost, cared for or mistreated as an infant. A steady stream of questions has been with me my entire life. How much was I held in my orphanage? What were the conditions that I was exposed to during my first year? Who took care of me? Was I cared for? What if I wasn't, then what? What if I had lasting effects that I never realized? Because I didn't know the answers to these questions and so many others, I wouldn't bake them into my origin story. This is why I started

SEE OUR LIVED IDENTITY

The identity we inherit.
The parts of us we are born with
and the culture we are born into.

List all of the parts of your identity that you inherited at birth. Now imagine that you are introducing yourself to a new neighbor for the first time.

- How do you respond to "Tell me about yourself"?

- Which parts of your Lived Identity are included in that introduction?

- Which parts are included if it were a new work colleague?

- Which parts are included if it were your boss?

By seeing which parts of your identity you lead with and the parts you struggle to share, you can begin to see which aspects of your Lived Identity you hide. This way, you can better see the power and privilege others may hold within an interaction.

my origin story in an airport. If I started it in Korea, it opened up a rabbit hole of conversations I didn't want to have with my coworkers or the barista at Starbucks on a Saturday afternoon. It wasn't a part of my identity that I saw as part of me.

Over time, though, I realized it wasn't the Korean side I was rejecting, it was the assumptions people were making about my origin story. Just by looking at me, they assumed they knew me. They saw a different story than the one I had experienced. They saw a narrative that they wanted to see, not me for the origin story I had actually lived. I let other people's biases define who I was and who I could become.

When I had my children, however, that changed. For the first time, I saw someone that looked like me. And when I looked at them, I could see parts of my Korean side. It was a profoundly human experience to look at this tiny human and see my al-mond eyes or my jet-black hair. Up until that point, I had never honored my true origin story. I had never seen anyone in the world that uniquely looked like me. But in my children I finally saw beauty in my Asian-ness and I could never unsee it. That was their inheritance. And it forever changed me. When I finally saw the beauty in this—in them—in me, I embarked on a journey to reclaim my authentic origin story. To see and truly embrace all of my Lived Identity. I was done hiding. I flew to Korea and began the search for my birth mother. I was on a mission.

• 5 •

Origin Stories

It's interesting how some words trigger us. Some words can even ignite a physical response in our bodies. For the longest time I bristled when I heard the words "orphan" or "adoptee." I could feel it in my body before I could process it in my mind. I hadn't taken the time to dissect my own origin story to find real beauty in my beginnings.

My life didn't begin at an airport like I had told people, like I sometimes told myself. My life began in Korea in postwar Seoul. There is little I know about the first year of my life. The details were sparse. Decades later, they're still sparse. I was found in a police box on the street when I was just a few months old. I was put into an orphanage, then a foster mother took care of me until I was adopted by a white, religious, midwestern American family. That was my origin story. The one that I had repeated over and over to friends and strangers. I didn't question any parts of it. I didn't try to understand anything beyond those few facts that had shaped a lifetime of pain. I just accepted them as truth. But that truth wasn't the whole story.

What We Inherit

For some people our origin story is recited like muscle memory, passed down from elders with rituals and celebrations. For others it is lost in the fog. And many times the more extreme our beginnings, the more we leave out descriptions of how our lives began.

Even though we cannot change our starting point, we can change our relationship with these aspects of our identity. I couldn't change the circumstances of what I was born into. This was my inheritance. These were the things that were given to me. I was born in Korea. I was born into poverty. I was given up by my birth mother. I was an adoptee. All of these things are part of who I am. I had to begin to accept that this was my starting point.

Homecoming

To go on this exploration of my origin story, I needed to fully see the culture that I was born into. To see the things that created the circumstances where single mothers had to leave their children in a police box. To see the system in place that made this not an exception but a common practice.

It's important to understand the context of the world I was born into, in postwar Korea. At the time there were more than two hundred thousand children being adopted and sent throughout the world from Korea—a number so large that Korea became known as the "Land of Orphans."[17] This massive number also means we, as adoptees, are a diaspora. A community so large that the Korean government funds visits called "Homeland Tours" for adoptees who want to return to the country that we were forced to leave so we can rediscover where we came from.

When I saw the beauty in my children and the Asian-ness that they had inherited, as well as how that part of me had become a part of them, I made the decision like thousands of other adoptees to return to Korea to attempt to learn the truth of my origin story. When I made that journey and arrived in Seoul, I was immersed in a place where everyone looked like me. At the same time, though, no one looked like me. I thought that for once in my life, I'd fit in. But that wasn't the case. I had never—nor have I ever—felt like more of an outsider as I did in Korea. One of the first places I visited was the adoption agency that had been responsible for me during those first months. I was brought into a room that was just big enough for me and my husband to sit down with the caseworker. The woman assigned to me started by sharing my adoption papers, and I noticed how thin the file was. It was light. There were only a few documents inside. This wasn't the start I was hoping for.

One thing that stood out, though, was a picture of me that had been stapled to the inside of the folder (see exhibit 2). I

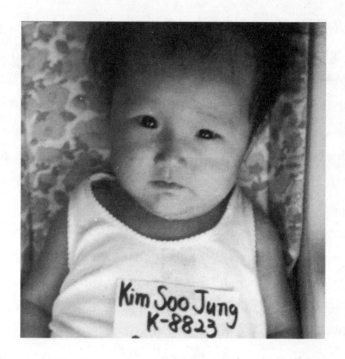

**EXHIBIT 2. First known photograph of the author,
Kim Dabbs, as an infant, 1975**

Source: Author's personal collection

was only a few months old in the photo, but I recognized myself
immediately and knew that look in my eyes. What held my attention the most was a small piece of paper pinned to my chest
with a number and case file written on it. The photo resembled
a mugshot. As the caseworker was reading the accompanying
police report, I couldn't hold back the sinking feeling that my
identity had been criminalized.

The police report had the address of where I was found and what I thought was very little else. But as we read the report together, there was one detail that immediately caught the attention of the woman assisting me. "This is unusual," she said. "It has a date and time of birth listed on the police report." That stopped both of us in our tracks. "How could a stranger know the time I was born?" I muttered under my breath, locking eyes with the caseworker. My head was spinning. She hadn't seen that before on a police report. There was another bread crumb of information in the document that made my heart skip a beat and stopped me for a moment from breathing all together. "This is odd," the caseworker softly said. "The name you were given is the same name of the person who said they had found you on the street."

"What does that mean?" I questioned, unable to fully process what I was being told. "Why would the person who found me and brought me to the police station give me her name?" The caseworker explained: "It could be that the very person who claimed to have found you is your mother. She would have known your birth date and the time you were born. And usually, they don't give the child a name, but she did. Instead of having the police station give you a generic name, it appears like she gave you her own family name."

I want to believe that my birth mother did this as a way to leave a clue for me to find in this search for my beginning. To one day find her during this journey to belonging. I used to think my life started in a box on the street. But what if I was wrong? What if my life started in the arms of my terrified mother who struggled to make it just like I did? What if with the barriers to success in front of her, she gave me the only thing she could—her name?

After a long search, I was never able to find my mother in Korea. But the clues she left sent me on a quest to better understand the culture she lived in and the culture I was born into. My origin story was impacted by the cultural policies in Korea that told women they couldn't be single parents. It was impacted by the mechanism that forced women to officially use the formal process of "abandonment" for their children to get rights as a Korean citizen. It was impacted by the bleak economic conditions in a postwar country. A country where leaving children in a police box wasn't a punishment but the only option single mothers had so their children could have some semblance of opportunity.

Seeing the structures and systems in place at the time allowed me to come at my origin story from a place of neutrality. *What if how I was born was enough?* I asked myself. *That I was equal? That being born female, Asian, and Korean was not a thing of shame but a thing of beauty? What if that was a gift and not a curse?*

I was finally seeing the power in my beginning. And it was a beginning born out of strength. I'm a fighter because I was born into a world that demanded it. I'm a fighter because it was my inheritance. I'm a fighter because I'm my mother's daughter.

Through this realization I began to see my Lived Identity. I began to find belonging within myself.

Build to Belong

I went on a Belonging Journey to see my Lived Identity by understanding the culture I was born into. The things I thought were fixed were actually fluid. The complexity came into full view once I could see these aspects of myself. I found the beauty in loving my origin story and learned to let go of those stories others had told me about who I am and where I belonged.

Maybe you have examined your starting point and don't like the circumstances you inherited. But knowing you were born worthy of belonging is key to being seen, heard, and valued on your own terms. Growing up, I introduced myself saying "I am American." Today I introduce myself as a Korean-born, American-adoptee, living in Germany. I learned how to see my identity and communicate how I see myself. Now it is time for you to define how you see yourself on your own terms. It is your turn to write your origin story. To begin your Belonging Journey, take time to see all of those things that you have inherited. Write down all the aspects of your Lived Identity such as your race, gender, ethnicity, nationality, socioeconomic class, and sexual orientation. Think about which of these aspects you claim.

To unearth the shifts we unconsciously make—or aspects we downplay or hide—imagine a time when you would introduce yourself to a friend, coworker, or stranger. Which parts

WRITE YOUR ORIGIN STORY

Take a moment to reflect on your own origin story. Write it out as a short story. Be as descriptive as possible about how your life began.

- Which parts of your Lived Identity did you claim?

- Which parts of your Lived Identity didn't show up in your origin story?

- Why is that?

Now imagine your same origin story rewritten with aspects of a Lived Identity that aren't your own to see how they would impact your opportunities in life.

- How would your origin story change if your gender or race were different?

- How would your origin story change if you swapped out other aspects of someone else's Lived Identity?

By exploring and interrogating the barriers to opportunity within the identities we and others inherit, we can better understand our relationship to the things we were born with and into.

of your origin story would you share? And which parts of your Lived Identity would show up in those introductions? Now take a moment to consider what a formal interaction would look like. How would a job interview go? How would you introduce yourself at a networking event? What about a team meeting? These types of questions can open a conversation that allows us to see ourselves and how we see our Lived Identity. It could be a subtle social cue that can show up in the signature line of our emails by including our pronouns. For some, it could be on your business card, and for others on social media profiles. We can ask ourselves why we lead with some things and not others? For example, do you share your pronouns in signature lines? Do you do this because it creates the conditions for you and others to be seen?

It is time to discover what your relationship with each of these aspects of yourself is and could be. To do this, trade out some of the aspects of your Lived Identity. For instance, when I swap out female with male or Asian with white, I can see the barriers that I have faced more clearly. These aspects of a Lived Identity would change the way I have experienced the world. And this is true for others. If the students where I began my career explored experiences with different identities, their daily lives would be different. But you have to see these things and make space for them. Weave that complexity into your origin story. Make space for the origin story of others. When I meet someone for the first time, instead of asking them where they are from or where they live, I like to ask "Where do you call home?"—that place that makes them feel safe. There is power in that. It is time to live your power.

· 6 ·

Learned Identity

The identity we choose.
The parts of us we have claimed.

One of the most important roles of parenting is ensuring our children have choices later in life. Do they have a choice to go to college? Do they have a choice in the career they pursue? Do they have a choice in where they want to live or how they want to express themselves? This is what parents work on every day: to help root our children in their identity so they can see the impact of their choices today, and how that shapes the choices they may have in the future. But this extends past being a parent. And it extends beyond our children. We all want choices.

For many of us this shows up in the jobs we pursue, the friends or partners we choose, and the educational path we explore. If I were born in Munich, the city I live in now, my choice of education would have looked very different from being born in Seoul or Detroit—or anywhere else in the world I've lived. I was raised in a system where higher education was a cost that was carried by students or family. My kids are growing up in a system in Germany where higher education is paid for by the collective. My career choices were very different from the choices they will have because of the culture I inherited and grew up in.

The path in front of each of us is paved by these past choices in our cultures that are enshrined in rituals or rights. But choices are complex. Some of them aren't that easy for us to see if they are the norm of the culture we live in. Education is a norm in many cultures, but it plays out in so many different ways. The right to an education. The right to an education as a female. The right to a free education. The right to a free higher education. These choices are directly linked to our Lived Identity that we have inherited. Gender impacts our choices. So does race, socioeconomic status, and so many other parts of our identity that we have inherited. All of these choices made in our cultures, however, could be tools for equitable access to opportunity.

At this intersection is where we find our Learned Identity.

Claim Your Learned Identity

Claiming our Learned Identity is the second step in the Belonging Journey. This entails the aspects of our identity that we've chosen, which include our profession, job titles, relationships, partners, education, and many other things where choice-making shows up in our lives. By working to understand and define our Learned Identity, we are able to better understand the choices we've made about who we are and who we want to become. By exploring what cultural norms are, how they show up in the choices we make, and how our Lived Identity underpins the choices we have in front of us, we can see the world more fully. We begin to see the choices we make as part of a complex system that is rarely an individual act of decision making, but instead a collective action shaped by the culture we live in.

The aspects of our Lived Identity may be difficult to claim, but they're easier to see. You know your race. You know the economic situation you were born into. You're taking the steps to better understand your origin story. Our Learned Identity, however, goes beyond that and is more complex because the choices we have in front of us are rooted in the Lived Identity we inherited. We inherit the norms and rituals from those before us, and because we don't live in isolation, we have to learn how to process all of those social cues and decide what to do with them. Our Learned Identity, though, is not only found in the career, relationship, and educational choices we make. It also shows up in the music we listen to and the clothes we wear—the artifacts of our identity that are shaped by our everyday decisions. Suit or T-shirt? Indie or classical? Bus or Benz?

But having the ability to make choices is a privilege. And the choices we have and our ease of exploring them is how we can see the systems that are set up for our success and where there are barriers to opportunity. This is where privilege shows up in our life. The choices we have made and those we have in front of us depend on an entire ecosystem of opportunity that is abundant for some and scarce for others. This ties into the lie of "bootstrapping it"; when I was leading a nonprofit organization for students from under-represented and under-resourced communities, I was told they'd be fine if they just "tried harder." And they'd be successful if they would just "pull themselves up by the bootstraps."

As I've already said, these attitudes sent me into a rage. When you don't have the lived experiences of the students who are forced to navigate the impacts of a system of oppression every day, it's easy to point at the person and not the barriers. We may like to believe we worked hard and "earned" our success. But the reality of the outcomes of bias within our systems is something we can't ignore. The National Bureau of Economic Research performed a study that demonstrates Black mothers and their babies, regardless of their income levels, have the worst childbirth outcomes in the United States. For example, in the state of California, where the study took place, for every 100,000 babies born to the richest white mothers, 173 die before their first birthday compared to 437 babies who are born to the richest Black mothers in the state and 653 to the poorest Black mothers.[18] This isn't just about wealth, it is about systemic failures from bias and race. So when we think we have choices or access to opportunity, that is a narrative that we have to interrogate more fully to get to the truth.[19]

But identities don't stop with individuals. Everything has an identity. Our teams do. Our organizations do. Our community does. We may not always see these things as having qualities that are inherited, but they are what underpins the rituals and norms that surrounded us every day. When we deconstruct and see these identities, the picture of the choices we make is fuller. For example, does your team meeting start with a cup of coffee or with a cup of tea? Do you have a timesheet, or do you have unlimited vacation days? What about your interactions and the language used; is it formal or informal? Is referring to a team member by Dr. or Ms. common practice, or do you use first names? Do you sit in individual offices, or do you sit together in a collaborative setting? Do you speak up, or do you have to wait to share ideas?

All of these aspects of the team become considerations for the choices we have in front of us. When we choose our Learned Identity, we are also choosing the identity of the teams we engage with. Those teams are shaped by the people designing the culture of an organization—and within those choices is where power and privilege reside. Just like us as individuals, sectors also have an identity. Corporate organizations do things one way while startups that were founded in a garage have their own way of doing things, and other sectors may be somewhere in the middle. There are command-and-control teams, and there are distributed teams. When we join a team, they have a Lived Identity already in place. So we spend some time trying to figure out where we just landed. For many people this is an uncomfortable journey.

When I chose to work in a century-old, American-owned manufacturing company that was founded in the Midwest, for instance, I had a bias that being "corporate" meant business attire, chain of command, and formal language. This was a stark contrast from when I worked in nonprofit organizations where people wore whatever they had available to them and addressed each other on a first-name basis because there wasn't an established hierarchy. Making the choice to "go corporate" was the opposite of everything I had believed to be true earlier in my career. Essentially I thought I was entering hostile territory. My beliefs about being a nonprofit organization meant that you were working to make the world a better place. That you were the ones righting wrongs. When I had to choose a career, I initially identified with fighting the system.

I didn't see it through that lens at the time, but when I chose the nonprofit organization, I was choosing a part of my own Learned Identity. I thought that being a fighter meant that I had to create an us versus them. And when people saw me, they saw the pieces of that identity, the choices I was making about the causes I cared about and who I chose to work with and for. It was an extension of who I was. But I ultimately realized that was a false choice. Change can happen anywhere. I saw a chance to make a difference no matter the sector, organization, or team I was a part of. When I worked in nonprofits, business leaders would give me advice on how to be more like a business. When I worked in business, nonprofits would give me advice on how to be more like a nonprofit. All I wanted to do was build a system that worked for everyone.

Challenge Norms

When we challenge the norms of our culture, centering ourselves in our Learned Identity helps us have clarity on our choices and the choices of those around us. But new choices demand new questions. We have to ask ourselves: *What do I want to fight for? Who do I want to fight beside?* The discovery of these two foundational questions can be a conscious choice, or it can be happenstance. When I met Alexandra Moldovan and Kinga Pakucs, two changemakers in Romania that I worked with in my role in social innovation, it was a mix of both. By claiming their Lived and Learned Identities, they were building a culture deeply rooted in providing a sense of belonging in a place where barriers to opportunity were the norm, both in the workplace and in the community.

Alexandra grew up just outside of Cluj, the second largest city in Romania during the midst of the fall of Communism. Throughout her upbringing, the culture Alexandra experienced was impacted heavily by a country that was grappling with its own identity. This made her journey of defining her own individual identity even more complex. Navigating systems where being under-resourced was the norm, health care was

challenging, and gender bias was prevalent, day in and day out,
Alexandra was confronted with choices that were already made
for her. She recounted the challenges in Romania in her childhood over the years we worked together. Having to use candles
because of lack of electricity and standing in food lines to get
rations was normal for much of the population, not the exception. Receiving two oranges at Christmas was a special treat, do-
mestic violence was commonplace, and the word "divorce" dare
not be uttered. Yet the new world Alexandra was beginning to
experience offered bold ideas that challenged the assumptions
she had about the world and what it could be.

When Alexandra was in the tenth grade, she discovered the
GLOW Camp (Girls Leading Our World), a program founded
by the United States Peace Corp rooted in girls discovering,
growing, and finding their voices. She credits these camps with
"saving" her. She found her own voice and discovered she had
the power to think for herself and be a conduit for change.
After this experience, Alexandra started to write in her high
school newspaper to amplify her voice, and she embraced
writing as her way of making a connection. Upon graduation
from high school, she moved to Cluj. In this more liberal
urban environment, she began to feel free of the burdens of
the past stories she had been told about who she was and who
she could become. "How does gender impact our decisions?"
she began asking. "Should women stay in the kitchen?" Depending on your experience, these may feel like questions

from a bygone era. But imagine growing up being told "Don't say no too often!" "Be a nice girl!" "Learn to cook because it's your place!" It becomes hard to know any other way, and this narrative still exists for girls and women in many parts of the world today.

Despite this exploration, by the time Alexandra entered the workforce, she still felt something was missing in her life. She asked herself: *What else?* The camp experience stayed with her, and she was looking for opportunities to get engaged in the community. When someone asked why Alexandra didn't start her own camp, it was her lightbulb moment. She began planning and connecting with colleagues to bring a new wave of opportunity into her community: she decided these camps would be her legacy to the world. Through the rallying of fellow employees and some seed money from the company, Camp Ignite was born. Alexandra had found her gift and she was sharing it with the world. It was all about choosing to use her voice and finding a vehicle for change. But now that she had clarity on what she was fighting for, the next thing she had to define was who she wanted to fight beside.

Unlike Alexandra, who grew up on the outskirts of a city, Kinga was raised in a small town by a Hungarian father and a Romanian mother. In that part of the country, Hungarians were the dominant majority, and they weren't afraid to demonstrate their power. Horror stories circulated from town to town of the ethnic traumas that had been committed on the Romanian people in the Hungarians' fight for independence. Despite the reality outside, though, Kinga's experience was that of a warm and loving family who looked after one another and cared for each other. She always felt a strong community bond. Though she didn't know it at the time, while waiting for a train at a station to go to a high school debate, Kinga had a conversation that would ultimately guide her choices for the rest of her life.

A young American man was lost at the train station, and after offering him a hand, Kinga learned he was with the Peace Corps. He invited Kinga to the GLOW camp he was working with. Despite the man being a complete stranger, Kinga, eager to experience the opportunity for herself, ran home and convinced her parents to let her go. During the camp her world was expanded. It was the first time she learned about gender equity, and she learned that she too had a voice and her input was valuable. Kinga started to speak up and speak out. She pursued a master's degree in gender studies and decided to find a way to serve the community.

Coincidentally Alexandra and Kinga worked in different departments at the same company. Their worlds collided one day when Kinga heard someone mention GLOW and was pointed in Alexandra's direction. The two immediately hugged and embraced each other over their shared love for the camp and all it had done for them. From that moment on they teamed up to work on Camp Ignite, work they've been doing ever since to create opportunities for teens throughout Romania to find their purpose and power in who they are and who they want to become.

Your Own Dream

Through Alexandra's and Kinga's experiences we can see the complexity in our choices. There is so much promise and progress in the movement they are creating for hundreds of teens throughout the country. Yet it can't be ignored that both of them were presented with a dream from another country. Each of them had an interaction with an American, something in a time of crisis in Romania they described as exposure to a "higher society." They perceived Americans as "weird alien saviors." By meeting the Americans through GLOW, both women felt intimidated as they gained glimpses into a different world—a real-life version of what they'd seen on TV. But after meeting Americans and experiencing the camp, they realized, for different reasons, it wasn't *their* dream. The Peace Corps and GLOW were the American version of a dream. Alexandra and Kinga knew that this was where both power and privilege showed up in their lives and in their country. And most important, they knew they didn't need to be "saved."

I asked them both what the Romanian Dream is—not the dream delivered by the West, but the dream that each of them have for themselves and their community. "I want to see a country where human rights are not debatable." Kinga took a long pause and continued: "I want to see a country where you don't have to leave the country to earn money or because of your sexuality. I want to see a country not surviving but able to thrive. A country where a cleaning lady can live. You know when you see retirees on their terrace smiling or enjoying their daily walk to get bread? I want to see that. A country where it's not hard to be old and a country where the elderly don't dress in all black and have their heads down."[20]

Alexandra saw Romania as a country marked by silence. "We have always been silent, and it is not in our human nature to be silent." She said: "For me, the Romanian Dream is getting out of this silence and having a civil society owning the narrative. We are a very reactive people due to Western influences and Communism. So my dream is to be free from this silence. This would lead to lessening of corruption at systemic and political levels and giving people the courage to actively be something instead of passively reacting to the norms. This could help stop the huge exodus that Romania is experiencing."[21]

The two changemakers have taken their dreams and together turned them into action. Through Camp Ignite they design and deliver experiences rooted in their Lived and Learned Identities. They created a new dream—a Romanian Dream—where young adults living throughout the country have a space to show up and be true to themselves, while at the same time also being vulnerable enough to express that to others. To create a safe space to maximize connection and ensure authenticity during the camp, guiding principles were established. Norms like "Not deciding who's wrong or right, but for people to get things right" and "We aren't here to judge at all but to support teenagers so they can express themselves and be respectful to each other while really expressing their thoughts and feelings."

Alexandra and Kinga saw the impact on their community and themselves, which gave them a renewed sense of purpose at work and in the community. The camp gave them such an emotional investment that was rooted in values and helping an unjust world to be more just. They began using business as a force for good, and they loved their choices. When others hold power instead of sharing it, they can make their own dreams or the dreams of their country the default for others. When the cultures tell you that you can't be authentic and you have to hide parts of your Lived Identity to be a part of that team, organization, or community, your choices disappear. And because of our fundamental yearning to belong, we change ourselves. Our clothes. The way we communicate. By masking the unique parts of our experience, our gifts become buried. And rather than claim our Learned Identity, we hide it because when our choices are taken from us, everything feels like a mandate not an invitation.

We have the opportunity to claim our Learned Identity for ourselves and create safe spaces for our teams, organizations, and communities to do the same. We can design the conditions for choices to thrive so that we can all thrive. This begins with naming when our aspirations and our actions experience a gap.

Belong to Yourself

Every single day we have choices in how we show up. We have choices in how we engage with the world and how the world engages with us. Ask yourself: *Are there policies in place accelerating or hindering my ability to have choices? Where can I remove those barriers to participation and use them as a tool to build equity into our world? What about with hiring practices? Do I look at the names and pictures on résumés, or do I prioritize the skills and abilities of the applicants?* When we see bias, we are able to remove it. For instance, did you know in job postings, the use of semicolon results in more male applicants? This means that when you are hiring someone on your team or in your organization, you have the opportunity to create more choices for more people by seeing the bias within systems and changing things, not just for yourself but for others, for all of us.

There are always "assisters" and "resisters" that can help you fully realize your identity. "Assisters" are people and policies that provide the freedom to have equitable access to opportunity. "Resisters" are those people or policies that consciously or subconsciously hold up old systems that work for some but not for all. And when we make space for the multitude of identities that exist and the assisters and resisters to opportunity for yourself and others, you begin to see the world more fully. You begin to see where you are able to let your own gifts—and the gifts of others—become unleashed. By fighting the system, not the people in it, we are able to build a more just and equitable world.

CLAIM OUR LEARNED IDENTITY

The identity we choose.
The parts of us we have claimed.

You need to live your own dream, not the dream that others have defined for you. It is time to name the things in your life that you want to fight for. List ten things that you care deeply about.

- Which ones do you choose to fight for?

- Who are the people you want to fight beside?

- How could that show up in your life? Your work? And your relationships?

The choices we have in life and how we claim the things we care about can be a strong guide to where we spend our time and energy. Gaining clarity on the topics that matter to us can be a consistent force in our lives.

And we do that not only for ourselves but for others along the way. There are so many choices that we can influence. There are so many barriers that we have created. Because of that, there are so many opportunities to ensure that people have choices in their lives as a right and not just as a privilege.

Now it is time in the Belonging Journey to examine your choices and to take inventory of your Learned Identity. We know what we have inherited; now it is time to share with others how the aspects of your identity you've chosen to claim shape how you experience the world every day. Start with your career, family, relationships, and education. When you define these as an extension of your origin stories, you will have a fuller picture of who you are and how you want to be seen, heard, and valued. How would any of those choices you have made (e.g., wife, mother, school, career) be different if your Lived Identity were changed? When you are able to see the ease or barriers of choices on different identities, it allows you to build empathy and understanding beyond your own lived experiences.

Think back again to how you would introduce yourself. Which of the traits you described are part of your Learned Identity? Some people lead with work titles, while others lead with educational achievement. Maybe for you, geography of where you live tops the list. And this could shift with the psychological safety of the audience. When we are with our neighbors, we may lead with our children, or partners, or even our pets. It is a different side of us that we want seen in those moments. And this has even more meaning when we are with friends or loved ones. It could be "extrovert" or "introvert" as we describe the parts of us that are so close to us, we sometimes forget to name them.

These stories we've been telling ourselves that don't serve us may be hard to edit, but we have the power to rewrite them. To create a new normal. To design new rituals that serve our Lived and Learned Identities for ourselves and others. But to do that, we must define for ourselves what we value.

• 7 •

Guiding Principles

When I was a teenager in the 1990s, the AIDS epidemic was ravaging the world. Instead of sitting on the sidelines, I was determined to do something—anything—to raise awareness in a time when so many people were choosing to look away. I began working as a volunteer for the AIDS Resource Center in my community, but it became evident pretty quickly that not enough people were listening to the movement. They turned it into an us-versus-them debate while people were dying in the wake of inaction. I kept asking myself, *What can I do? What change could I effect when the power to change things is held by adults?*

The Center invited me to go along with them on their bus trip to Washington, DC, to see the AIDS memorial quilt laid out in its entirety at the National Mall. Cleve Jones, a San Francisco resident who lost a friend to the epidemic, began the quilt when painting the name of his friend on a single piece of fabric.[22]

Over the years more than a hundred thousand names were added to the NAMES Project's AIDS Memorial Quilt—names of sons, daughters, mothers, fathers, neighbors, coworkers, and friends. It was tragic. And powerful. Jones had ignited a revolution through art resulting in social change in his attempt—and the multitude of supporters of the project—to make visible the names of those whom society was ignoring. I saw the power of collective impact. I knew I could do more.

When I got back home to Michigan, I started volunteering as an HIV and AIDS educator for teens through Planned Parenthood. My role was to share information and resources for my schoolmates and friends to be aware of the issues. I also provided tools for them to protect themselves. One of those tools was free condoms. Let me repeat that—*free* condoms. This may not seem like a crime today, and some of us wouldn't even blink an eye over it. But in a small midwestern conservative community in the 1990s, it was as if I had a scarlet letter on my chest. The moment my school found out, they expelled me. Livid, I did what I thought was right at that moment: I contacted the American Civil Liberties Union (ACLU). I asked them to advocate alongside me to amplify my voice and share that this cultural norm needed challenging. No matter the recourse or punishment that was handed down, I was determined not to be silenced—because I knew silence was at the heart of this epidemic that was killing people. The ALCU stood next to me in my fight for my rights in that situation. The school issued an apology and allowed me to return. Through that experience I discovered the power of collective impact.

I had pulled at a system that worked for some but not for all. And it changed me forever. Every system is like a rubber band. When you pull at it, you know that it's going to snap back, and when that happens, the snap stings. My school snapped back when they expelled me. And that moment stung. But I was standing up for the rights of others in a time when too many people were turning their back on them. Even though the terms "equity" and "belonging" weren't yet part of my everyday vocabulary at that stage of my life, they had already been rooted in my values and actions. Those experiences built the guiding principles I formed over a lifetime. Having the ACLU by my side gave me the courage to keep standing. But there have been countless times when I stood up to power without anyone beside me, whether in the workplace or in the community. By rooting myself in my values of equity and belonging, I wanted to ensure that when I was pulling on those old systems of power and privilege, I could stand firmly no matter how hard the system came snapping back at me.

Claim Your Values

Many of us spend our lives longing to sit at someone else's table. We feel that we have to work hard to "earn" the right to be with others and to have our voices heard. Even when we are "granted" a seat at that table, sometimes we start to change who we are in an effort to be seen, heard, or valued on the terms of those seated before us, not our own terms. When we define our values, however, we no longer accept environments where we feel forced to conform to others' ideas of what's "acceptable." We are done hiding aspects of our identity because we are grounded in knowing we are worthy of being seen, heard, and valued on our own terms.

We do this by believing in our worthiness, and we accomplish that by rooting ourselves in our individual values. When we have seen and claimed our Lived and Learned Identities about who we are and how we are showing up in the world, we not only live our values authentically and with purpose, but we ensure the lived and learned experiences of ourselves and others are honored in everyday interactions. Belonging is a practice, not a solution. It is something that we have to revisit day after day, meeting after meeting, and conversation after conversation. It is something that we may feel amazing at one day and need reminding of on others. When we have the clarity of how we see, hear, and value ourselves, we turn this into the habits and norms of our everyday lives.

Design Your Guiding Principles

When we design how we want to show up in the world, it is a unique mix of aspiration and reflection. During the initial stages of my own Belonging Journey, I kept a notebook full of reflections that outlined all of the aspects I wanted to ensure I was being true to in my own Loved Identity—a practice I still do today. I continually ask myself, *If I am a fighter, what are the themes of my life that would help me stand firm when my values are pressure-tested?* Some of the guiding principles I created were based on things that I've practiced over and over throughout my life whether in meeting rooms, in the principal's office, or even in taxi cabs at the airport. When I gave words to these principles, and kept them front and center, it guided me in those inevitable situations. I practice these daily in both good times and bad times.

When rooted in your own values, this reflection of designing your guiding principles should bring you great joy. These are the moments when your aspirations and actions are in line with what you stand for. The moments you are true to yourself. The moments when you live authentically and fight for what you believe in and it fills you with purpose.

Below I share my own seven guiding principles for belonging. They are unique to me, and they aren't for everyone. These insights, however, are the foundation for how I ground myself when I feel like an outsider. My go-to's in difficult situations. A way for me to make choices that align with my values at home, at work, and in the community. In addition to defining my own guiding principles, I've borrowed from other people who have inspired me by their words or actions during my Belonging Journey. When I heard these guiding principles, they stayed with me. I would keep them in notebooks and put them on Post-it

Notes on my office whiteboard. I would repeat them when I was in conversation or giving talks. I knew these guiding principles were lasting actions for me to uphold, and they have become part of my daily practice.

Speak truth to power. Speak up when you hear or see injustice in action. This is the ultimate fight-or-flight moment. Every time it happens to me or others, I feel my blood pressure rise. The world slows down. Rooms fall silent. And I muster all that I have at this moment to lean into my values. I need to speak the truth. The hard truth.

When we only call people out, though, we don't allow the space for growth or change to happen. When we leverage shame as a tool of power, that doesn't shift hearts and minds toward belonging. It pushes us further into our corners and ensures that the us-versus-them mentality wins the day. We must have enough humility to understand that our truth is not the only truth, and we need to leave the space to listen with the same intensity with which we want to be heard.

Use power to share power. Paulo Freire, author of *The Pedagogy of the Oppressed*, wrote back in the 1960s: "In order for this struggle to have meaning, the oppressed must not, in seeking to regain their humanity (which is a way to create it), become in turn oppressors of the oppressors, but rather restorers of the humanity of both."[23] These words still hold true today.

All of us have a gift to share with the world, which means all of us have power. And the only purpose of power is to share it with others and create the space for others to do the same. This is what creates a diverse, equitable, and inclusive world where everyone can feel that they belong.

It is easy to live in an echo chamber when you are surrounded by sameness. If you create a culture that only hears you, or sees you, it is another signal that the power you have isn't being shared with others. We need to listen first to understand and then wield the power we do have to create space for others. Because that is where justice is rooted and when we restore humanity for everyone.

Act with bravery. This is one of my guiding principles because I've often felt like I was risk-averse. But when looking back on my life, I realized that belief was in direct conflict with my actions. I have lived a life of great bravery, but I hadn't always held those beliefs close to me—the times when I didn't have the benefit of knowing the outcome and I moved forward anyway.

I have climbed the Himalayas, and I have jumped out of airplanes. I have moved to a country where I didn't know the language, and I have taken jobs where I don't know the sector. I have had tough conversations with friends, and I have had to walk away from situations where I wasn't being respected. I have had to crawl out of bed from the depths of depression, and I have had to show up in places where there was no one like me. And sometimes I have had to say no. And saying no is sometimes the greatest act of bravery we can exercise.

This usually shows up in those quiet unsuspecting moments. You are sipping coffee with a friend or in a virtual meeting and someone says something that doesn't honor the humanity of others. It is in that moment that bravery is required, no matter the outcome. Acting brave, however, isn't calling them out, it's calling them in, in a way that also recognizes their humanity. In those moments, speaking up is harder than any mountain I've climbed or plane I've jumped out of. Regardless, we must act bravely.

Impact over ego. So often we make decisions through a biased lens, which is so hard to see when we are doing it. I lead with this guiding principle because it serves as a constant reminder that bias is a battle, and our ego will try to make us do things that aren't aligned to our values.

When making a decision, big or small, I always ground myself by asking: "Is this decision based on the impact it will have or is it based on my ego?" This serves as a filter check on critical choice points because the ego is sneaky, and I try to be intentional with the choices I am making. I ask myself, *Is it the dopamine hit, or is it the accountability to the people, team, or community that I serve?* Doing so keeps me grounded in my values.

"Do or do not, there is no try." —Yoda. If you aren't into *Star Wars*, this one won't embed itself as deep in your heart as it has in mine. It's been a guiding principle of mine for decades. I have been relentless in my approaches to things because I go all in on the things I decide to do. We've all been in those planning meetings with the guise of "trying." This usually consists of people throwing out lots of ideas that include lots of barriers, and before we know it, the clock expires and people move on to their next meeting. And with all of that "trying," nothing moves forward. When people come back together and wonder why an approach didn't work, they say, "Well, we tried!"

I would rather put something half-baked into the world than nothing at all. Because each of those small attempts move the needle, and the culmination of those acts builds a movement.

"Be for each other." —Hatch. At the heart of this guiding principle, whether during tense moments in meetings or everyday conversations, is that you can disagree—radically disagree. But you must communicate in a way that sees the person who stands before you as worthy and honors their humanity. You must be for their success. And you must come at it from a place of empathy.

When I want to radically call someone out instead of calling them in, this guiding principle comes to the front of my mind. I remind myself that what I am going to say and how I frame it has to be in service of me wanting this person to succeed. To give them the space to be their authentic self with the empathy to deliver it in a way that honors their humanity. This guiding principle is grounded in the simple reminder that "I am *for* them."

"I am here to get it right, not to be right." —Brené Brown.
I couldn't have this list of guiding principles without including
Brené Brown. She's been such a beacon to this work and a
source of inspiration on creating cultures of belonging for so
many people in the world. When she said, "I am here to get it
right, not to be right" on her podcast *Unlocking Us,* it stuck with
me.[24] It lodged itself in my heart, and when I feel that my ego
is starting to eclipse my desire for impact, I go back into these
words and recite them over, and over, and over again.

These seven guiding principles for belonging have become the
choice-making framework that allowed me to unleash the gifts
I bring to the world. When faced with situations where you
want to live in your full Loved Identity, your own principles are
what can guide you into being seen, heard, and valued on your
own terms. Words without action are just aspirations. Defining
your guiding principles and practicing them when your values
get pressure-tested allows you to turn them into action every
single day. To embed guiding principles into your Belonging
Journey, we go back to our Lived and Learned Identities. We
recite our origin story to see our full selves, not the stories
others have written for us. We share the choices that we have
claimed in our lives in a way that honors our experiences. Because when we define how we value ourselves, we stand firmly
in knowing that this is how we can connect to purpose in our
lives.

YOUR OWN GUIDING PRINCIPLES

What are some of the guiding principles that best reflect who you are and how you show up in the world?

- Which statements guide your choices?

- Which ones do you want to amplify?

- Which ones do you want to shift?

- What are the values of those you work for and with?

- How do they align with your own?

The more clarity we have on the things that guide the choices we make in life, the better we are able to see, hear, and value ourselves in any situation.

As you root yourself in the values that you live by to ensure that your identity is honored, you will see patterns emerge: Insights of how you have lived your life and the soundtrack of statements that are running in the back of your mind. These guiding principles that you define serve as a reminder that you belong in every situation. This is because you belong to yourself—and you see, hear, and value yourself on your own terms. Designing your guiding principles should be the part of your journey that is done with ease and excitement. It is when you synthesize the patterns in your life that bring you joy and you carry them with you as some of your proudest moments. The times when you feel most like yourself. When your words and actions are in line with your aspirations. Maybe you haven't distilled them down into easy-to-remember one-liners, but this practice should give you great pride and energy.

Your Turn

By doing the work in this chapter, we have outlined how to live our values by creating the guiding principles of how we want to engage with the world. Now that we have the tools for choice-making in our daily life, we have to listen deeply to the voice that shapes the narrative about who we are—our inner voice. When we understand the stories we tell ourselves about who we are and where we belong, we can better create a safe space for ourselves within our own lives. It is time to examine the words we use that are critical in creating the conditions for us to thrive. Reflect upon your go-to stories throughout your life. Remember how you showed up in those moments. What did you do? What did you say? When you think of the takeaway as you tell those stories to others, what is the lasting lesson?

Being an advocate and organizer was a story from my youth. And there are several others that I've repeated over time. This was when "speaking truth to power" and "acting with bravery" showed up in my early years. They were easy for me to pinpoint. These were the moments when I embraced my Lived and Learned Identities. Now it is your turn.

· 8 ·

Lingering Identity

The identity we default to.
The old stories we tell ourselves
about who we are and what we deserve.

Whenever I am being othered, for some reason, the experience with the airport taxi driver plays on repeat in my head. You could have traded out the taxi driver with any number of people that I have interacted with throughout my life, from meeting rooms to train platforms. "Where are you *really* from?" This question has been asked in more introductions than I care to count. There are entire YouTube channels dedicated to these types of microaggressions. These tiny paper cuts that add up over a lifetime have the power to bleed you dry. The internal pain I felt when triggered by the taxi driver wanted to play itself out as being so perfectly passive-aggressive that he'd have no recourse but to give up asking questions.

But he didn't. And I didn't. I had a choice at that moment. I could stop the conversation short with "Why do you ask?" Or I could ignore the question entirely. But I felt compelled to be a complex mixture of nice and exasperated all at the same time. I internalized it. And that pain lingered for years. The thing about pain, though, is that it can be contagious. When people are hurt, they are prone to hurt other people. They bring it with them into other aspects of their life whether at home, work, or in society. We need to edit this vicious cycle. I could continue to allow the taxi driver to dominate the story I told myself, or I could choose to let it fuel different parts of the things in my life that I wanted to fight for—the things I cared about. I chose to make a commitment to edit the story I told myself to leave this cycle of pain behind.

Edit Your Lingering Identity

Our Lingering Identity is our default position that's rooted in old stories we tell ourselves about who we are and what we deserve. It's hardwired into our brains and impacts how we respond under stress. It shows up in situations where we feel like an outsider, and we fall back into those old habits as a survival mechanism. In these situations your guiding principles are a critical tool. They serve as your north star to help you stand firm when your values are pressure-tested so you can find the power of being seen, heard, and valued on your own terms. You've been practicing this as you've explored your Lived and Learned

Identities through this Belonging Journey. Now is the time to take this into the outside world. It's time to turn these learnings into practice when you feel like an outsider.

In the instances when we feel our Lingering Identity driving our internal narrative, instead of suppression or avoidance, to reset our sympathetic nervous system, neuroscience shows us we need to practice acceptance.[25] In order to practice this acceptance, we need to examine the moments and circumstances when we feel like an outsider. These moments leave clues that allow us to understand why we feel the way we do. Once we identify which environments and circumstances trigger our brain into survival mode, we can lean into our guiding principles. Ultimately, as we turn to them, we're able to sunset the stories that aren't serving us as we're making decisions based on our values and choosing how we want to show up in the world.

The Belonging Journey is a tool that you can use in any situation, whether at work, home, or in society. Use it like a reset button when your Lingering Identity shows up and tries to override your inner truth. It has multiple benefits when you are forced into stress mode. It slows you down enough to get your brain to pause. That alone—taking a step back to pause to reset—is a win. That pause will shift you from the back of the "survival" brain to the front of the "logical" brain. It has the power to pop you out of survival mode when your brain is set on autopilot with the old stories you tell yourself. This pause will give you a pathway for seeing what's possible in the situations when you feel like an outsider. It provides the space for you to turn to your guiding principles when it's hard to stop your thoughts so you can respond on your own terms. Each of the steps we walk ourselves through to edit our Lingering Identity is important. These steps help to root yourself in your authentic self so you can make values-aligned decisions.

This Is Your Brain on Autopilot

The human brain is a wondrous thing. But like all wonders, it's extremely complex. It has the ability to click into survival or protection mode and is hardwired for risk aversion as it scans the environment to identify either enhancements or impediments to our lives. This predictive coding may keep us safe in some situations. But like all paradoxes, if it gets set in a loop full of biases, it becomes hard to slow down much less change.[26] When this happens, the brain goes on autopilot. It takes the shortcut of accepting information without examining why we are doing something or why we view ourselves and others the way we do. It's like a toddler learning to walk. After those first few steps the brain doesn't consciously tell you to put one foot in front of the other. It just puts one foot in front of the other.

The same holds true with the story our Lingering Identity tells us. When we continually feed ourselves these false narratives about the strength and resilience of who we are—*I'm too loud* or *I'm not quiet enough*—we slowly set the stories we tell ourselves into stone. The initial trauma from those narratives of *I'm too this* and *I'm not that* compound to create trauma on top of trauma. We build this mental model that we automatically operate out of, and we stop questioning if they have truth or if they are productive. As those stones stack and pile on each other, our brain stops actively looking for new stories and narratives to exist in that space because it's packed with the old stories.

Change, however, is possible. We have the ability to reset and rewire our brain. To take the experiences that our brain has used as a mechanism for trauma and build fresh connections and forge new neural pathways. These bias loops and habits rooted in the stories that aren't serving us can be broken. We can accomplish this by seeing the stories we tell ourselves and rewriting them in a way that authentically serves us. There is a name for this: neuroplasticity. According to researchers Matt Puderbaugh and Prabhu D. Emmady, "neuroplasticity, also known as neural plasticity or brain plasticity, is a process that involves adaptive structural and functional changes to the brain."[27] Or as scientist Christopher Bergland has noted: "One could speculate that this process opens up the possibility to reinvent yourself and move away from the status quo or to overcome past traumatic events that evoke anxiety and stress. Hardwired fear-based memories often lead to avoidance behaviors that can hold you back from living your life to the fullest."[28]

Now is the time to heal from those stories, to sunset them and leave them behind. In order to do this, we need to identify our triggers during the moments that make us feel like outsiders.

The moments when our values are pressure-tested and we struggle to define how we want to be seen, heard, and valued on our own terms. When we do this, we're able to regain choice in our lives. It allows us to respond in a way that is authentic to our identity and both our own humanity and the humanity of others. For example, let's consider the woman I interviewed who had been ridiculed by some of her classmates because her school lunch consisted of food from her culture, like dumplings and chicken feet. She carried that pain of exclusion with her for years. However, today, rather than feel shame and embarrassment, she edited her relationship with the food of her culture and started a business selling these very items at events and conferences to share her pride with others. Instead of internalizing the feelings of being less than, she used them as a differentiator, something that made her special. And she brought that to the world.

Triggers + Response

I'm too Asian. I'm too outspoken. I'm not nice enough. I'm not quiet enough. My entire childhood was filled with stories where I told myself I'm too much of one thing or not enough of another. When I began my career, the pattern accelerated. And as much as I didn't want to believe it, the social cues of others reinforced these sound bites in my head. It was exhausting. I didn't realize it at the time, but I was operating in a constant state of burnout. But this wasn't caused by my workload, it was caused by the stories I told myself and feeling like I didn't belong. I bought into the narrative of the stories I repeated in my head.

As they stacked, these narratives added up to me believing I wasn't enough as I was. This made me feel like even more of an outsider because I felt like I didn't belong to others or myself. And I allowed the opinions and stories of what other people said about me and the expectations of society to compound this feeling.

"You should smile more."

"You shouldn't be so assertive."

"Your delivery is too direct."

"Your English is really good!"

Stories hold tremendous power. No stories, however, are more powerful than the ones we tell ourselves. What initially begins as just a thought, over time as the stories repeat, turns into a deep-seated belief about who we are and what we're capable of achieving. The stories I told myself became the person I saw when I looked at myself in the mirror. I realized these stories needed to be edited.

To sunset the stories that weren't serving me, the first thing I needed to do was understand my triggers and responses. In psychology a "trigger" is defined as a stimulus that causes the painful memory of a traumatic event to resurface.[29] These triggers can show up in any number of situations and stimuli, ranging from specific places that remind us of traumatic events to something we hear, see, smell, a certain time of the day or year, and yes, even a taxi driver. A common example of a trigger is the sound of fireworks for military veterans with post-traumatic stress disorder (PTSD).[30] A certain type of dog might be a trigger for a person who was bitten as a child or the sound of a school bell for someone who experienced trauma in school.

What I realized over time was that my trigger was rooted in the times I was being othered. My Lingering Identity would show up when I wasn't being seen, heard, or valued. Since this happened all the time, my body was operating in a constant state of trauma. It was why I felt constantly exhausted. It was literally wearing me down. Tiny paper cuts that add up over a lifetime have the power to bleed you dry. I felt literally sick and tired of feeling sick and tired. To begin to rectify this and understand my own triggers, I needed to go through the Belonging Journey to see my Lived Identity and to claim my Learned Identity. By practicing my guiding principles, I could more clearly understand what was happening in those moments, which offered the opportunity to edit my Lingering Identity.

When feeling othered or facing a situation that caused us trauma in the past, the body can see and feel it before the brain does. Our breath changes. Our heart rate spikes. Our palms may begin to sweat or our stomach may begin to tighten. When we recognize this is happening, that moment is an opportunity to revisit our guiding principles as we can make the choice to respond with intention and not just reaction. The words "adoptee" and "orphan" are a trigger for me. They bring up past traumatic experiences and memories. My body sends a shot of pain as my brain scrambles to process what's happening while simultaneously going into protection mode.

With varying degrees, we've all experienced this feeling at some point in our lives. Situations where your body shouts *run* and your brain follows. By asking yourself, *What are my triggers?* you are taking a critical step in knowing how to engage the Belonging Journey because it allows you to begin to edit the stories that aren't serving you. When we are feeling othered or experiencing stress, our negative thoughts cause this stress to compound. As you encounter these situations, take note of when and where they are most prevalent in your life to identify which specific instances and environments trigger you. The more clarity we have regarding the source, the more effectively we can design a response on our own terms.

One tool that has served me well when responding to these triggers has been asking myself these three questions so I am rooted in belonging.

1. **Am I safe?** This is where we recognize and understand that we are being triggered, which is a critical first step in regaining agency. While our bodies are feeling the fight-or-flight emotions, it allows us to create a pause where we can observe the circumstances that led us to feel like an outsider as well as the associated emotions that come with it. By questioning if real danger is imminent, it grounds us back in a place of safety to better process what is happening.

EDIT OUR LINGERING IDENTITY

The identity we default to.
The old stories we tell ourselves
about who we are and what we deserve.

The *I'm too* myth is hard to break. To reset these stories, you have to know where they show up over and over in your life.

- What are the *I'm too* stories you tell yourself?

- When do they show up?

- What are the situations or triggers before your inner voice says *I'm too*...?

In the moments when my Lingering Identity shows up, I have three questions that I turn to. Now design your own three questions that you can ask yourself that provide you with the space to reclaim agency and respond authentically.

2. **Is it real?** As we step back, we allow ourselves to claim the power of choice. The important thing is not to suppress our emotions but rather to learn from them as they hold vital clues and information as to why we feel a certain way. This pause gives us a chance to interrogate whether what is happening is real or perceived.

3. **Am I responding with humanity?** We can't control the
   actions of others, but we can control how we respond.
   Once we have seen the trigger and claimed the power
   of choice, we can respond in a way that is aligned with
   our guiding principles. This isn't about being "nice" but
   about being honest and honoring the humanity of others.
   Doing so builds a bridge to understanding.

Give yourself the space to engage the Belonging Journey to
guide you through how you want to show up in any situation.
This response is a tool for how to engage in the moment. Think
of it as a ritual that allows you to pause to edit your Lingering Identity as it allows you to regain agency and the power of
choice. You may not always get it right, as disrupting this cycle
and rewiring your response isn't easy. But by seeing the triggers
and taking these steps, you can create a new default response
that reflects how you want to be seen, heard, and valued on your
own terms.

Pressing Reset

We all have stories that we tell ourselves that are rooted in old
beliefs and narratives that others have written for us. Many of
us lead with the story of what we *aren't*, rather than who we *are*.
For some, the consistent narrative beats to the drum of *I'm not
professional enough*. For others, the stories that show up again
and again are *I'm not resilient enough* or *I'm too quiet*. Maybe your

I'm too's are something similar because you feel as if you're not worthy or enough as you are. Or maybe they consist of a long list of things you don't even realize you are saying or doing.

Rather than experiencing the pain of being an outsider, we respond by changing ourselves to adapt to our environment. We change our language, our clothes, or other cultural cues that are part of our Lived and Learned Identities until we reach a point where this response becomes ingrained and automatic as a survival mechanism. Sometimes, without even realizing it, as these stories compound and our responses become reactionary instead of intentional, we can lose our identity along the way. The *I'm too* and *I'm not* stories we tell ourselves can be hard to edit. However, by identifying these specific triggers and doing the work of resetting our Lingering Identity, we can sunset the stories that aren't serving us and step into ones that do.

• 9 •

Sunset Old Stories

Ti Chang has spent her entire life feeling like an outsider. When she was six years old, her family moved from Taiwan to a predominantly white, middle-class, Christian town in Georgia, a state in the Deep South of the United States. From day one, it was clear to Ti that people treated her as the other. Everywhere she turned, whether through overt racial slurs to covert social cues, she was reminded that she was less than. And it wasn't just strangers. Ti's parents taught her to play by the rules and to never ever speak up or stand out. Ti was forced to grow up fast. During the week, all through high school, while her classmates were playing little league and taking dance classes, she took care of her three younger siblings while her parents worked. And on the weekends, while her classmates were attending parties, Ti worked at her parent's furniture business in an under-resourced part of town that was a hub for other immigrant families.

She found sanctuary, however, in her art. It was the one place where she could authentically express herself, and it was one of the only safe spaces she encountered in school. To avoid the pain of having to eat lunch alone in the cafeteria, as her classmates didn't want to sit with her, Ti hung out in the art studio. The art teacher had opened their door and allowed Ti sanctuary—something that three decades later still lights her up. But despite Ti's obvious passion and talent, pursuing art was not an option and viable career path in the eyes of her parents. She was told they didn't make the sacrifices they'd made for her to become a "starving artist."

But Ti found a loophole. After getting a scholarship to Georgia Tech, she studied industrial design as a way to honor her parents yet express herself creatively. Unfortunately there wasn't a loophole for exclusion. When she began her career, in each company she worked for, the feelings of othering continued. "Many companies have every intention of trying to create a table for people, but ultimately, when a company lacks diversity, it just doesn't happen," she told me. "I was the first woman hired at Goodie as well as the first industrial designer, and at Trek, I was the first woman hired out of thirteen designers."[31] Ti constantly felt like she had to prove to her male counterparts that her work was valuable and worthy of consideration.

After her successes at Trek and Goodie, where Ti designed one of Goodie's highest-selling products, she wanted to learn more and continue to grow as a designer so she applied to study at the Royal Academy of Arts in London (RCA). Hoping to find equity and education in this new path, Ti again faced exclusion and experienced disappointment. Through previous work experience, she uncovered a passion for designing products for women. But when she expressed this ambition to her adviser at RCA, he shut her down and said he'd ask her to leave the program if she pursued that focus and body of work. Despite being threatened with flunking out two more times by her professors after challenging the status quo, Ti adapted herself to their rules and did the necessary work to graduate by designing objects they required—a far cry from her dreams of innovation and empowerment. By the time Ti left London, she'd slid into a massive depression, unsure of how she wanted to move forward.

For Ti, the systems she encountered everywhere she went influenced the story she told herself regarding her worth. *I'm too introverted. I'm too sensitive. I'm not friendly enough. I'm too emotional.* And it hurt.

Rewrite Your Narrative

We all have stories that we tell ourselves. Many of these stories are rooted in old beliefs and narratives that others have written for us. So many of us lead with the story of what we *aren't* rather than who we *are*. We tell ourselves, *I'm too this* and *I'm not that.*

But are we? Rather than repeating the stories that we tell ourselves, we can question them. We need to see what these stories are and why they were written that way. Once we begin to see the mantras that are holding us back, we have to ask ourselves, *What proof is there that has convinced me this is a fact?* To find this proof, we have to look at and dissect the cultural context by asking ourselves if the story we're telling ourselves is one that we've written or one the world has written for us.

For Ti, during her childhood and throughout her twenties and thirties, being an outsider and the exclusion she experienced caused her a lot of pain. But it wasn't only because of overt racism or sexism. As an introvert, she was often made to feel by society like there was something wrong with her. The world presents healthy humans as extroverts, someone with lots of friends. On top of this, as an artistic soul with a passion for designing products for women, Ti was told she was too sensitive and too emotional. As these experiences stacked, she bought into the societal narrative that this combination made her weak and not deserving of a seat at the table. We may not look at it through a cultural or systemic lens. But when we dive into why we feel like an outsider, the root of many of these stories we tell ourselves has little to do with us and everything to do with systems that have been created for some but not all to thrive. To sunset the stories that aren't serving us and to authentically step into the narratives that do, we must question these systems. We must redirect them to lead with who we *are*, not who we *aren't*.

It's not uncommon in the social impact space to hear the words "we do this *for* people." Though well-intentioned, social change needs to be rooted in working *with* people. It's a small shift in language but a huge shift in approach. You don't fix people. Only you have the power to fix you. You can, however, fix broken systems. Similarly, during my work in the community early in my career, some people saw the students I was working with through a lens of who they weren't and what they didn't have. But rather than allow the narrative of "help these children in need," we flipped the language and focused on the narrative of "creating a culture of opportunity with students by removing barriers to social and economic progress in their lives and community."

This change in language changed everything. Instead of encouraging people to see our kids as people that needed saving, we centered on the systems that needed changing. We wanted people to be motivated to take action because they saw the beauty in our students and their gifts that were laying under the surface, waiting to be unleashed. People lined up at the door to see what they could do to be a part of this movement to change the systems that were the barrier to progress in the students' lives.

I've seen this time and time again. I brought these same approaches to the corporate sector. When working through our social innovation and impact strategy, one of the ways we were able to design *with*—and not *for*—community was by shifting our language to match our intentions. I brought Trabian Shorters in to work with our leadership team. CEO of BMe Community, an award-winning network of innovators, leaders, and champions

who invest in aspiring communities, Trabian has been instru-
mental in advancing this cause through work he coined "asset
framing." This movement focuses on "equity without stigma."

Rather than placing the impact of systemic failures on the
individual, Trabian roots the mission in leading with assets, aspirations, and contributions to change the narrative and spotlight
the truth. His work is explained well in the *Chronicle of Philanthropy*. Society reinforces a narrative around Black communities
in the United States that minimizes the assets they hold and
amplifies the deficits they are associated with. "This is not
only insulting, it's inaccurate and ineffective," Trabian noted.
"Eighty-two percent of black men in America are not poor, and
57 percent are solidly middle class. They serve our country in
uniform at the highest rates and are the most actively engaged
fathers in the nation, according to federal statistics. So why does
philanthropy only convey the image that they are absent or a
problem or a threat?" He added: "You can't lift people up by
putting them down."[32]

We can do the same as individuals. We can rewrite our stories. We can lead with the assets we hold and not the deficits
we've told ourselves about our worth. We can edit our Lingering
Identity. Framing is about which information we choose to lead
with. Leading with our assets becomes very difficult, however, if
we see ourselves through the lens of who we're not or what we
don't have. Instead, we must view ourselves through the lens of
who we are and what we do have.

We are the authors—and therefore the editors—of our own story. We get to choose what we focus on and lead with. When we edit our Lingering Identity, we view ourselves through a lens of our value and the gifts we are sharing. This helps us break the stories we tell ourselves when we feel like an outsider. Rather than look to the outside world for a sense of belonging, we are rooted in the fact we already belong to ourselves because we are worthy and we have gifts to share.

Radical Reframe

After graduating from RCA, which hurt Ti's creative confidence, she bounced around jobs and over time, by doing the necessary inner work, she allowed herself to play again. She thought about what she really wanted to do and uncovered her passion—designing products for women—which she felt that RCA tried to bury. If that was going to happen, she'd have to go at it alone.

Like so many people, Ti used the Covid quarantine to press reset. While doing this work, she changed the frame in which she saw herself. Rather than allow the story of *I'm too introverted, I'm too emotional,* and *I'm too sensitive* to dominate her internal narrative and dictate her worth, Ti began to embrace these characteristics for the gifts that they are. "I got very comfortable being an outsider," she told me. "Not having a lot of friends, I didn't have the peer pressure of people telling me that I shouldn't pursue designing pleasure products for women. If I'd had that, I feel like I would have lost my voice, but instead, I followed my own moral compass. As I've gotten older, I realize that's just who I am."

Ti recognized the power in being emotional and that being sensitive is her strength. Whenever her Lingering Identity shows up or someone flat-out says, "You're too sensitive," she remembers, "Yeah, of course I fucking am. That is what makes my work good. It's how I create beauty. It's because I actually fucking care." One of her motivators today is to ensure she articulates that in some way to the next generation of designers. There are a lot of people who are sensitive like her, and they get lost in the shuffle as people bulldoze them and think they are weak. But through her journey, Ti's grounded in the fact that if you can harness that care, you can make something truly beautiful.[33]

Retire Your Too's

Although my stories of *I'm too this or too that* were different from Ti's, the steps I took to own my narrative and not reach for a mask in order to fit into the rooms I walked into were similar. I had to question the stories I told myself to get to the heart of who I am and what I stand for. By taking the time to explore my Lived and Learned Identities and focusing on doing the work to edit my Lingering Identity, I could see all the pieces of my identity I wanted to start to weave together as a whole. Through this process I had a breakthrough moment.

I've spent my entire life and the entirety of my career fighting for others. I use my voice and platform to make that happen.

SUNSET OLD STORIES

Introduce yourself to yourself as if you were your own biggest fan.

- What would your biggest fan say about you?

- How would they describe you?

- What qualities would they highlight?

Your biggest fan may just find that your *I'm too this or too that*, which you used to see as your kryptonite, could be your superpower.

I'm relentless in my pursuit, and I'm always challenging systems. For the longest time, due to my fight, I thought I couldn't also be a lover. I thought it was one or the other. And the stories I told myself reinforced this narrative. But I *could* be both. I *am* both. I am a lover *and* a fighter. Hell, my fight is rooted in love.

This is my narrative. I own it. Me and me alone. Since I've chosen this path, I must also create the conditions for others to do the same. To listen to others with the same intensity that I want to be heard. To see others with the same intensity that I want to be seen. And to value others with the same intensity that I want to be valued.

Each of us has the choice to write our own story. To stop letting the world tell us who we are and to begin telling the world who we are. When we do this, we define how we want to be seen, heard, and valued in a way that gives us a sense of belonging in any situation. When we embrace this, anything and everything becomes possible. We know who we are and we are clear on the person we are striving to become. The goal is progress, not perfection.

But to do this for yourself, to sunset the stories that aren't serving you and step into the ones that do, you need to get clear on the *I'm too this* and *I'm not that* stories that you say about yourself. You must edit your response and ultimately retire these narratives.

Where do your "too's" show up in your life? Where do you feel less than? Where do you feel like you aren't enough? The times when you feel like you aren't worthy of being your authentic self or your authentic self isn't worthy of being loved? This shows up when we feel like an outsider looking in at everyone who appears to have figured their lives out. But what would happen if you decided to write your own story? If you saw yourself for all the things you hold instead of all the things you want to hide? When you lead with your assets and sunset the stories that are not serving you, you can author ones that do.

These stories may be hard to edit. But that's the work. We get to choose our path. There isn't a path more worthy of a fight than taking the steps to belong to yourself no matter the situation. When we see our Lived Identity, claim our Learned Identity, and edit our Lingering Identity, we take the last step in our Belonging Journey and own our Loved Identity.

• 10 •

Loved Identity

Our authentic identity.
The power of being seen, heard, and valued
on our own terms.

Being a fighter was both my inheritance and my choice. For years I grappled with this part of me. It felt like a curse. For decades I chose to hide it. To be nice. To not make a scene. But by choosing to be nice and to hide, I was not being kind to myself and others. By denying my identity, I became a watered-down version of myself. Less than. Filtered. Like an outsider.

I needed to see that *I am who I am.* I needed to internalize that the culmination of all my experiences helped make me, me. Beautiful experiences. Heartbreaking experiences. The more I explored my Lived, Learned, and Lingering Identities, the more I realized fighting wasn't just an inheritance and a choice, it was my purpose. It was a part of me that I wanted to share with others. I wanted to find a way to ground myself in that strength and use it to fight systems that worked for some but not for all. To create cultures of belonging where everyone can thrive.

That was my fight. That realization brought me to the identity I loved. It was also the part of me that could change the world. In order to do that though, I had to stand tall when I felt small. I had to change systems and bend them toward justice when others disagreed. Most important, I had to create the space for others to do the same. But this realization wasn't some kumbaya moment. This moment was a revolution. When you live with radical authenticity, you find your power—the power you hold that is unique to you. There is nothing more thrilling than that discovery. When you find your power, you find your purpose. And when you live your purpose, that is at the heart of belonging everywhere.

Own Your Loved Identity

We now take the next step in our Belonging Journey by learning how to own our Loved Identity. It is in this step—when we understand our origin story, question the systems that create the conditions for us to make choices, and claim the parts of our identity that serve us and discard those that don't—that we live with authenticity and find unconditional belonging.

Our Loved Identity is our center. It is where we bring our best version of ourselves to the world while allowing others to do the same. It keeps us moving forward rather than allowing others to define when and where we belong. It holds our aspirations so we are able to see, hear, and value ourselves on our own terms. When we do this, we can stand firm in any situation because we know we belong to ourselves. We're not going to get it right every single day, but our Loved Identity gives us clarity on the person we are and who we want to be. It's time to lead with that, not hide it. It's time to find our power and love who we are and how we show up in the world. This is the most crucial yet most challenging step in your Belonging Journey because it transforms you into someone who makes decisions grounded in knowing you belong here. By doing so, rather than looking for a seat at someone else's table, you build a new table where your Lived, Learned, and Lingering Identities transform into one you Love.

Earlier in the book we met Daniel, who traveled the world and worked through the struggle of trying to understand what binds us together as humans. He discovered that what unites us is finding and giving the gifts that we all hold. He rooted himself in the humanity we all share. By doing so, Daniel created safe spaces for others to do the same. He created a community of belonging where everyone could thrive in some of the world's most challenging conditions.

We also met Yodit, whose experience of being othered and feeling the pain of exclusion enabled her to see the aspects of her Lived Identity as well as the systems that denied her humanity because of that identity. However, rather than allow the world to tell her when and where she belongs, Yodit used her Lived

Identity as a force for good by building a movement around radically reimagining systems that don't just work for some but work for all.

Alexandra and Kinga claimed their Learned Identities and made choices to bring their whole selves to their work and their community. They began making choices where they didn't have to change who they are, and they told the world the vision of a future that they dreamed of. A dream that they had and could share with others. They built a new table because the one built for them didn't honor their lived and learned experiences. And now they get to share that table with young people throughout their country.

Ti found that her *I'm too this or too that* beliefs were actually her superpower and not her kryptonite. Rather than allow the world and her Lingering Identity to silence her artistic soul and the very qualities that made her beautiful, Ti was able to sunset the stories that weren't serving her and rewrite ones that do. Today, no matter the situation, she shows up as her authentic self. She's found her power. And she's using that power to empower others to embrace the parts of themselves that make them beautiful.

We all know the feeling of being an outsider: When we walk into a room and say to ourselves, *I don't belong here.* When we are forced to adapt to our surroundings, we suppress our uniqueness. If we can identify the circumstances when that happens, we can see all the barriers that brought us on our journey. When we go on this journey to understand our past experiences and the systemic barriers to entry, we can design our own future—a future rooted in our Loved Identity. As we fully leverage this and live with authenticity and purpose, we can be seen, heard, and valued in a way that gives us a sense of belonging in any situation—at home, at work, or in society. For example, when I saw myself as born into the arms of a caring mother, in a world that consists of systems that meant caring for me was letting me go, my eyes opened. I could then dive into the hard truths. I asked myself: *What if how I was born was enough? That I was equal. That being born female, Asian, or American didn't shape the beliefs of otherness that I would live in my life.*

When we go on the journey to understand how our Lived and Learned Identities have shaped us, we begin to see the choices that we made in our lives. We are coming to terms with the lived part of our identity. By seeing the structures and systems and coming at them from a place of neutrality, we begin to truly see ourselves. And seeing is believing in who you are at your core.

Stand on Our Own

In today's hyperconnected world of digital likes and faux approval, we need to learn to stand on our own. To understand that joy can happen without an audience. To define who we are and how we show up. Then we have to love that identity deeply. We must own our journey. We must control the choices we make.

If you want to be seen, heard, and valued, you own how you define that. You can design how you communicate that to others. Through an introduction or a social cue, the way that it is shared is a way that you have been clear in what that means to you. At the same time, understand that this may mean different things to different people. We all have a different starting point. We all prioritize different things in our identity. But we don't all have the privilege of being in safe spaces where we thrive. So think intentionally about how you want to share that. Because if you can't claim it, others will find a way to claim it for you (and you may not agree with the story they say about you).

Before we start looking for our own love in all the wrong places, we need to start within. Your inherited Lived Identity is part of who you are. You need to see that as a part of you that you love. You may not love the systemic barriers to entry, but you can love the parts of you that you've inherited.

To **see** the beauty in your origins.

To **hear** that voice inside repeating that you were born worthy.

To **value** the fact that you belong here.

And to do all of that on your own terms because you and you alone have defined that.

I love that I am a fighter. I love that I can claim that I come from a mother who I believe is a fighter. I have claimed that as part of who I am. While I used to think this was my kryptonite, I now see it as my superpower. You claim your Learned Identity.

But it is not something that is fixed as you can start to make new choices at any point in your life. New choices that are aligned with the identity you love. Begin to seek out places where your Lived Identity is honored. But you must first name those parts that matter to you and you alone must do that. For instance, I thought I would be a nonprofit leader for life. I had chosen that as my path. But lives and circumstances change. And the more complex we learn the world is, the more we understand that choices aren't linear. Now I am a corporate leader. Both positions share the same north star: fighting for equitable systems for people to belong and thrive in. My sector and job titles weren't fixed, but what I've chosen to fight for was.

We have all had that moment in our lives where we feel like our best self. When we learned something new. When we conquered fear. It is those moments that we need to catalog and claim. The insights that we learn about ourselves can clarify a pattern of our Loved Identity, a pattern we love and want to amplify. This is because when we fight for ourselves and our Loved Identity, we know we belong anywhere.

We need to start with ourselves and believe in our Loved Identity. Often the choices available and the systems calibrated for us can make us feel like the other. But we are all outsiders. The discovery of that unites us all. But you have to be the one to claim your identity. To change the systems. To find your power. To share your gift. Don't live someone else's vision of who you are. You choose the path. You own the journey.

A Revolutionary Act

Belonging to yourself is a revolutionary act. And with anything that is radical, many times it starts with a revolt. When we get to this stage of the journey, we begin to find comfort in the identity we love. Love is a journey full of peaks and valleys. This is the "forever work." A journey that is complex and beautiful and full of tears and triumphs. But we can all fight for love, and fighting for our Loved Identity is a fight worth having.

Shannon Cohen knew how to fight and she knew how to love—and that fight for love has been a catalyst for a movement. She moved from Detroit to western Michigan the day after September 11, 2001, eager to build relationship capital and meet other leaders and difference-makers. Shannon got involved in the networking and event scene, but time and time again, she was not only the lone Black person in attendance, she was also the only woman in the room and often the youngest. *Does anyone notice this?* she asked herself. *Does anyone care?*[34] The stark realization was that the answer felt like a no.

In an interview Shannon described the emotional labor you experience when you're an *only* in a room. How do you figure out ways to be yourself and not shrink? "If you've never been in that position," she told me, "you don't understand how that chronic discomfort feels." It's not just being in the room, she explained, but the internal churn and conversation angst that you experience just to show up. "Do I wear braids or use a straightener because of my layered hair? Should I wear heels? I'm already taller than a lot of people; do I really want to stand out even more? What about my big earrings that I love so much? Are they *too* much?" She wondered about what to wear and how to do her hair, questioning if those choices would somehow diminish her efficacy—or the assumptions of her efficacy—as a leader and a difference-maker.

What Shannon felt was not unique. A *Harvard Business Review* article from May 2023, shared a Crown Workplace research study that showed "Black women's hair was two-and-a-half times more likely to be perceived as unprofessional, and one-fifth of the Black women surveyed between the ages of 25 and 34 had been sent home from work because of their hair."[35] To add to her lingering unease, Shannon knew once she arrived at the networking event, she'd be photographed for promotional material so organizers could check the box to demonstrate the diversity of their attendees. One of those photos from an event dating back to 2016 of Shannon and her then two-year-old son is still used today by an organization to advertise their events. This suggests the organization has not yet done the work. When Shannon first saw the years-old image of her and her son, still in diapers at the time, she laughed out of bewilderment and disbelief.

As these experiences stacked, with Shannon having to carry the mental, emotional, and physical armor to feel like she had a seat at the table, it took its toll. Her tipping point took place during one event when she asked the organizer if they even saw this reality. Shannon pulled out a napkin and began to map out her dream for what that table would look like. A table that didn't feel so alienating, that caused people social anxiety, and that demanded a navy-blue suit to feel like they were worthy and belonged. A table that looked like Shannon's diverse friend group and resembled her own life. A table where women could come as they are and not feel like they need to put on the armor that they've picked up along the way from the spaces where they were othered or felt invisible. A table where there's no need for that armor to begin with.

Shannon turned that dream into a reality. The Rockstar Women's Movement started as a local movement of pioneer women who are "rocks" in their families, marketplaces, and communities whose lives have become the pavement for someone else to walk through. The movement has gone global. Shannon's consistently sold-out events since 2018 are multiracial, multiethnic, and multigenerational. And making these safe spaces for women to heal, explore, and have a place where their voices are heard and their experiences validated has made Shannon very proud. "As a builder and a binder," she told me, "I think that part of the reason that we've needed safe spaces is first to repair and to bind up broken hearts. There's been a lot of people that have been walking wounded in corporate spaces because of the weathering that othering and not belonging causes on those who wear that mantle of first—what a faith leader in my world calls 'the Ministry of First,' where there is no other example. Where their life becomes the pavement for someone else."[36]

But with great visibility, comes great scrutiny. Every change-maker I have talked to has referenced the system snapping back, what Shannon refers to as "sharp elbows"—a term she picked up from her friend that speaks to the passive-aggressive jabs that come with doing this work. When those who could have enacted change stay on the sidelines, but now that some-one else is doing something when they've done nothing, they feel threatened and make their power known. Shannon spoke to the many blessings that come from doing this work and how even though we celebrate firsts, we don't acknowledge the pain that it takes to pioneer a path, the burdens to carry. "There are some days that are really hard because construction is messy and the build process always precedes the ribbon cutting. But nobody really wants to talk to you before the ribbon cutting. But if you don't make it through the build process and the messy spaces of construction—including within yourself—you never get to the ribbon cutting."

What keeps Shannon going and so many others like her is she knows this work will outlive her. She knows that this is a season of innovation, not duplication. Through rooting her fight in love, Shannon owns her Loved Identity. And on the hard days, when she's building while navigating sharp elbows and her Lin-gering Identity makes her feel like wavering, Shannon looks at the pictures of the women she serves—pioneers just like her who are on a mission to pave the way for others—and she gets back up, dusts herself off, and gets back to work. This is her choice. And she loves the choices she's made.

Belong to Yourself, Discover Others

It is time to embrace what we have inherited and love the choices we have made and are going to make in the future. No matter the outcome. The revolutionary act of belonging to yourself begins with the audacity to get it wrong, brush ourselves off, and do it all over again. If you want to be seen, heard, and valued by others, you need to first see, hear, and value yourself. For me, this realization was a wake-up call. And every day, I carry that forward. Some days I get it right. Some days I get it wrong. Like, *really* wrong. But I keep going back to my core, reminding myself about who I am and what I am fighting for, and I start again. Loving your identity is one of the greatest revolutionary acts one can take. When we can see the systems for all of their inequities and see ourselves for all of our strengths, loving your identity becomes a tool not just for authenticity, it becomes a conduit for social change. Just like fear, love is also contagious. And both loving and fighting can live together in the same space.

By choosing to fight the system, I chose love. By choosing to stop letting the words of others cut me, I chose love. By choosing to design what I fought for, I chose love. When I feel like an outsider and my identity gets pressure-tested, now I tell myself: *You Belong Here.* That is what I am fighting for. And the community

OWN OUR LOVED IDENTITY

Our authentic identity.
The power of being seen, heard,
and valued on our own terms.

A motto I carry with me in my own life is "You Belong Here." Create your own motto about who you are and how your Loved Identity shows up in the world.

- When you read through it, does it make your heart skip a beat?

- Do you feel it in your bones?

Now take inventory of the interactions and choices you made when you owned your Loved Identity and felt that you showed up as your authentic self.

- What are the words that you would describe yourself as in these instances?

- In your teams in the workplace, what are the moments where you were able to come as you are?

- In your community, what are the situations where you felt valued for just being you?

Look for the patterns that emerge and take that into the world through your words and actions.

I am building around belonging is who I am fighting beside. I have left behind the stories I told myself about where I belonged. Today, I know I belong. This shows up in how I create possibility and opportunity in the world. That is my power. I am using that power to share power with others.

I don't have all the solutions, but I will always believe that change is possible. Day after day, accepting myself for who I am. This is a way to fight the overwhelming pressure of the world asking me to be like them. The oppressive culture of sameness. I make sure to look at the situation in the larger context and root it in reality. The journey is leaning into what you feel is right in how you see, hear, and value yourself. And not accepting anything less.

I am a lover *and* I am a fighter. I own my Loved Identity.

One of the greatest gifts we receive when we go on this Belonging Journey is our eyes open to the humanity of those around us. When we find belonging within ourselves, we discover others. When we live with authenticity, we want those around us to do the same. Our default position becomes one of curiosity instead of judgment. We see them through a more empathetic lens and begin to understand how to honor their humanity. To own your Loved Identity, you reconcile your Lived, Learned, and Lingering Identities with the aspiration of being seen, heard, and valued on your own terms. This means that you see what you've inherited and the world you are born into, you've claimed your choices, and you've edited the stories you have told yourself about who you are and where you belong. When you can do this, you own your Loved Identity and can stand firm in any situation. Which parts of your Lived and Learned Identities do you believe in and are willing to fight for?

When we know how we want to be seen, heard, and valued on our own terms, some of the ways to make it visible are the social cues that we can share with others that ensure they honor our Loved Identity. It could be adding your pronouns to your social media profiles or email signature. It could be leading with where you were born or where you now call home. Or maybe it is ensuring that the names of others are honored and pronounced with care. This is where you turn that anxiety into self-acceptance. When you can, you begin to live a different story—your story. A story rooted in an identity you love.

Do the choices you make for your friends shift? Your job? Your neighborhood?

We all have the power to define who we are. We also have the power to create the space for others to love their identity with the same intensity as you want to love your own. One of the greatest opportunities to ensure that happens every day, instead of accepting a seat at someone else's table where we have to mask our true selves, is to build a new table.

• 11 •

Build a New Table

We all have power.
Now is the time that we share that power
with others.

We've all experienced moments when we felt like an outsider. Moments when we are standing outside a room where we think we want a seat at the table. Sometimes we are even invited to sit down. But once seated, it's clear the table wasn't set equitably. At best, these tables can be performative or transactional and at worst, toxic. We feel the stares. Our voice is silenced. We're interrupted. We're talked over. Or we're invited to take a seat at the table and no one even looks in our direction. It is clear that these environments weren't made for us to show up, let alone show up as our authentic selves. As our stomach drops and our amygdala fires up, we question if we are here so someone can check a box. In those moments we realize that these tables are not calibrated for belonging.

When we own our Loved Identity, however, we step into our unique power. In doing so, our eyes open to the power that others hold and whether they decide to continue to hold their power or share it with others. When we define how we see, hear, and value ourselves, we want others to do the same. We want to build tables and create cultures for everyone to show up authentically. We accomplish this by designing safe spaces for everyone to come as they are. But this does not mean we need to be surrounded by others who are just like us. It's about creating cultures where people can bring their own Loved Identity to the world. It is where opposing viewpoints are welcome to ensure civil discourse and authentic interactions. It is where we honor the identities of others without compromising our own.

This is how we build belonging. It is how community thrives. It is how we become catalysts for change. When each of us can come as we are, we swap out pain for progress.

By going on the Belonging Journey detailed throughout this book, you have found your power and have the tools to stand strong in your Loved Identity when you feel like an outsider. It is time to decide how you are going to share your gift with the world while providing the space for others to do the same. Now is the time to define who we are fighting beside. If the table isn't set for belonging, it is time to **build a new table**—a table that's not just built for a select few to thrive but for everyone. Belonging is realized when we understand *everyone* is an outsider, and it's the power of creating space for those differences that unites us all.

A Table Set for Everyone

As human beings, we are deeply conditioned to provide a sense of belonging for others.[37] It's in our DNA, and we can leverage that force of nature to build with others to create community. We can do so in a way in which community is built for connection, not exclusion. But when we don't break this us-versus-them cycle, we perpetuate the crisis we are living in.

Community is about building for belonging. It's about knowing your own unique power of your Loved Identity and then creating spaces for others to do the same. The work of women inside the Obama administration allowed us to see the power of building a new table. In a *Washington Post* piece journalist Juliet Eilperin shared how Obama was the first president who claimed himself as a feminist. Within his administration he created the most diverse inner circle of any president to date. He filled the majority of his cabinet seats with women and people of color. But even still, it wasn't enough because the women continued to be and feel overshadowed by their male counterparts. To combat this, and create belonging for all not for some, these women made an "amplification" pact where they would raise each other's voices. As Eilperin explained in the piece:

> When President Obama took office, two-thirds of his top aides were men. Women complained of having to elbow their way into important meetings. And when they got in, their voices were sometimes ignored. So female staffers

adopted a meeting strategy they called "amplification":
When a woman made a key point, other women would
repeat it, giving credit to its author. This forced the men
in the room to recognize the contribution—and denied
them the chance to claim the idea as their own. "We just
started doing it, and made a purpose of doing it. It was
an everyday thing," said one former Obama aide who
requested anonymity to speak frankly. Obama noticed,
she and others said, and began calling more often on
women and junior aides.[38]

The amplification pact worked. When Obama began his second
term, Eilperin noted, women finally gained parity with men in
Obama's inner circle.

Obviously, this strategy can work for women beyond places
of extraordinary political power. I've witnessed it in countless
tables throughout the duration of my career. Research shows
time and time again that women are interrupted, talked over,
given less credit, or shut down significantly more often than
men—and women are penalized for this "behavior."[39] Clearly
this frustrating phenomenon doesn't only happen to women.
When you layer on the various Lived and Learned Identities, the
effects are even more pronounced. We need safe spaces where
people can come as their authentic selves. To do that, we need
to co-create the norms of the culture as well as rituals—like the

"amplification" pact—to reinforce these norms in a way that allows everyone to bring their unique identities to the table.

When we show up in places we feel we don't belong, we can leverage our own Belonging Journey to see, claim, edit, and own our identities so we can build a new table for everyone. Opportunity can be infinite. There is scarcity of access to opportunity, but the more stories we can honor and the more identities we can lift up, the more abundant opportunity becomes. When we do this at the community level, people can meaningfully participate in an identity they love. In this way sharing our unique power unleashes belonging for all. But because we don't live in a silo, we have to intentionally create space.

Safe Spaces Create Belonging

The term "safe spaces" can be a bit misleading. The word "safe" does not mean fluffy and nice. Creating safe spaces is about designing with intention. It means we can raise difficult topics and have tough conversations in a way that doesn't dehumanize but instead allows each of us to lead with our humanity and authenticity.

Civil discourse is a cornerstone of building safe spaces, and in an us-versus-them world, this critical skill is necessary to thrive. When you see where someone else's viewpoints are rooted, you can observe the social cues of belonging. These are the things we do that are unspoken. They can be overt or covert, and they are powerful signals for others. This shows up in code-switching at work—a term that describes the way that many of us have to change our language and other aspects of our identity to make others more comfortable in shared places.[40] But when we change our language, our clothes, and even our names, we mask our identity, and when we do that, we deny our own humanity.

These tables weren't built for people like Beca Velázquez-Publes, a community leader in Michigan who is changing the fabric of an entire community.[41] A proud Detroiter, Beca's origin story began in the southwest side of the city with a rich Puerto Rican and Mexican heritage. Immersed in the multicultural environment that had strong Latinx, Middle Eastern, and Black community representation, what *wasn't* present was equitable access to opportunity. This lack of opportunity carried forward into the workplace. When Beca worked in a predominantly white organization, she'd go into the office and feel abused. She left meetings completely demoralized as she got talked over and literally told to go to the corner while seated at tables she has been "invited" to join. She couldn't bring her authentic self to these tables. As a young professional, navigating this reality was isolating and demoralizing. No one prepares you for *that* experience.

When I interviewed Beca, she spoke about her experience moving to western Michigan from Detroit in 2008. In this environment you couldn't say words like "equity" and "race"—and you sure couldn't say "white supremacy culture." Due to the frustration of not being able to name any of those things she was experiencing, combined with watching how people inter-acted with her—being booed out of rooms or being told she's got a "hot Latina temper"—Beca said to herself, *This just can't be. There's something that can't be okay about this.* She knew she couldn't be the only one who had this feeling. In that moment she knew this table wasn't set for her. It was time she built a new one. But she didn't just build a new table, Beca built a movement.

It started with small things, like inviting a group of people throughout the community to informal gatherings. They cen-tered the experience on discussing why people weren't openly talking about race and equity and shared ways to start to nor-malize this conversation. As word of these gatherings spread, the size of these events grew. What started as a few friends, turned into a community-wide conversation as the attendees brought the language and concepts back to their organizations. And those concepts became policies. And those policies became practice. And that practice created opportunity.

Building a new table, however, doesn't mean we stay silent in the spaces where we don't feel seen, heard, and valued; sometimes the work is to reset the table that currently exists. This allows us to build a bridge to connection when we feel like outsiders to ensure we stand strong in our Loved Identity while creating the space for others to do the same. For Beca, having the confidence to have these conversations in the workplace is an ongoing practice. Repeatedly she found herself sitting at

tables that weren't set for her voice to be heard and valued.
It was transactional. She was invited to so many places just so
organizations could say they invited her. To combat this and
stand strong in her Loved Identity, before sitting at someone
else's table, Beca needs to make sure it is a safe space for herself
and others. She accomplishes this by establishing the norm of
asking herself three very specific questions.

- What power do I have when I sit down?

- How is my voice being used?

- Can I bring somebody with me?

These questions ensure the safety of Beca and others. It gives
space to ensure that people are seen, heard, and valued on their
own terms. When you give yourself permission to question the
table, the setting, and who is invited, you see the possibilities for
a more equitable path forward that is rooted in belonging.

Rituals and Norms

Each of us brings our own unique set of values to others. These
are things that we don't leave at the door as we enter new spaces
and encounter new experiences. We have defined our personal
values and the guiding principles that bring them to life. Because we don't live in isolation, now is the time to make space
to create collective values that are critical in building thriving
communities. As a practice at work, we have built norms into

the teams I lead. This practice ensures that everyone is seen, heard, and valued in the way that has meaning to them. We kick off with a norm-building workshop that takes our team members through the collective identity we co-design, while gaining a deeper understanding for each of us as individuals.

We define the areas in which we want to root ourselves by sharing our individual principles before designing rituals for how we want to show up for each other—given how each of us has defined and shared our unique identities. We do this through how we communicate and make decisions. Then we see how we respond when we are in challenging situations. By defining these norms up front, we can ensure that we have created safe spaces for each other to thrive. We synthesize these into a group norm set that can be used as our collective agreements. We lead with these norms at our weekly meetings. This creates the space to acknowledge how our norms showed up during the week and the areas we need support from each other. We ask questions like "How did these norms show up this week?" or "Which norms are you struggling with right now?" These regular pulse checks keep these norms top of mind for the team and each other. This practice has transformed the way we create the space for dialog, culture, and practice at work.

On a larger scale in my work at Steelcase, as we explore the future of work and create cultures of belonging where innovation can thrive, we looked at how we could design leadership spaces with intention. Instead of being on the top floor of a building behind security and protocols, we moved our CEO and senior leadership team to the first floor in the flow of foot traffic. We did this because we know that trust is built by proximity. By knowing that everyone had access to leaders, we leveraged space to let everyone know in the organization they were with us, not away from us. That was the social cue. And we created rituals to ensure these norms were honored. Rituals make our cultural norms a regular and repeated practice. Maybe your ritual shows up as morning coffee, a check-in, or the things you do to see others and to raise your collective voices. To amplify each other's ideas. To say, "You matter." Is it the afternoon walk or the virtual meeting? Is it the monthly sharing of celebrations? Or is it an annual retreat?

I recently connected with Bernad Ochieng Ojwang, who served as the Head of People and Belonging at Alight, a global organization that exists to "channel the idealism and goodwill of every person."[42] He developed a belonging practice by asking a simple question: "How might we foster a sense of true belonging?"[43] The resulting insights reinforced the need for rituals and norms that were co-created with the people that the organization partnered with. Although his team members didn't live in the refugee camps where they served, they discovered that the building of team norms was one way of creating safe spaces to begin and end their days. They used their commute time together to and from their work to acknowledge power dynamics. The power that was held in the world was building

BUILD A NEW TABLE

Take a moment to think about a time when people gather in your life. Maybe it is a meeting at work or a dinner with a loved one.

- How might you leverage the power of rituals to build a new table together?

- What is a quick way to redesign gatherings with them?

- When you are invited to a table that wasn't set for you, what are three questions you can ask to ensure you can come as you are?

Designing a filter check through these three questions, you have something to ground yourself in that you can either hold close or share to ensure you belong to yourself in any situation.

barriers to progress by diminishing the power of others because it was unequally distributed. This created scarcity of opportunity. Ojwang's team members used the daily commute time to find ways to use what power they had to unleash the abundance of the people everywhere.

In my own life I created belonging retreats for leaders who are on the front lines of change. These BEtreats are an intensive journey where leaders come together to discover their Loved Identity and bring it to the world. I built this experience to give people the space to step away from everyday life and focus on doing the necessary inner work to belong to themselves. Part of that is also designing rituals for when we step back into the world. We find accountability partners, supporters, and a network of people who are fighting beside us at a new table set for belonging. What interactions are needed to create a foundation of trust? At home? At work? In your community? A foundation that allows you to weave together your Lived, Learned, and Lingering Identities into an identity you love? How will you communicate that to those around you while making space for them to do the same? When we honor our humanity and the humanity of others, we are all able to come as we are.

CONCLUSION

Come as You Are

I've always felt the most human when surrounded by others who are being their most human. Their raw selves. Untethered. Authentic.

I see this most often in moments of sadness, joy, despair, and celebration. In rituals and at moments of extremes. Weddings. Births. Funerals. These are the moments when we feel humanity at its essence. When we feel community. It is with tears and triumphs that we become one. But community doesn't only have to live in the extremes. When we find our Loved Identity, we are able to witness community every day. When we do that, we see others' humanity in all its forms. And when we can see that, it says *You Belong Here*, because when you do, *I* belong here too.

Saidah Nash Carter, a researcher in South Africa, introduced me to an African concept called Ubuntu, meaning "I am because you are." Nelson Mandela described this concept: "A traveler through a country would stop at a village and he didn't have to ask for food or for water. Once he stops, the people give him food, entertain him. That is one aspect of Ubuntu, but it will have various aspects. Ubuntu does not mean that people should not enrich themselves. The question therefore is: Are you going to do so in order to enable the community around you to be able to improve?"[44] If you belong to yourself, what is it in service of if not for the collective?

Back in the spring of 2020, the beginning of the Covid quarantines in Europe, people sat on their balconies, craving human connection. They used the ritual of creating music together at the same time every night. And it went viral. When people saw this ritual, it reminded us that it wasn't exclusion that was uniting us but our inherent desire for connection. These are the goosebumps moments. The moments where you say, people truly are wondrous. Those moments are measured by the feeling. That deep feeling that brings you to tears. The hope you feel in the pit of your stomach. You know when you feel humanity. So many people focus on what their purpose in life is without knowing who they are, without loving their identity.

We are living in a volatile and uncertain world. But the next generation is not only aware of the issues that face us, they are also acting on them. Young people are rising to the challenges we are facing. And they are doing it together. In my work in social impact, I describe it as seeing the worst of human behavior balanced out by seeing infinite hope. There are so many people trying to right the wrongs of society, and that collective impact gives me momentum to know that change is possible. Building belonging is an invitation to a conversation. People's stories of belonging can unite us instead of divide us. Our experiences are uniquely ours. And it is in sharing the beauty and the struggle that we build community. Communities rooted in belonging.

I often give speeches on belonging for individuals, teams, and organizations. While sharing the Belonging Journey, I wasn't fully prepared for the conversations that happened after. Conversations full of people's experiences of exclusion and trauma. Full of pain. Full of hope. It was through those moments that I have built this body of work so that everyone can start to heal from the lifetime of pain that they have endured. When we suppress our humanity, it makes us feel less than. When we suppress our humanity, we don't belong to ourselves and we can't discover others.

These are the moments that rob us of joy.

These are the instances that deprive us of sharing our gifts.

These are the times where our purpose is marginalized.

Through this Belonging Journey, you have been able to see your Lived Identity and what you have inherited. You have claimed your Learned Identity and more fully understood the choices and systemic barriers in front of you. You have edited your Lingering Identity by sunsetting old stories that weren't serving you and rewriting ones that do. And you now own your

Loved Identity. You know how to stand on your own and see, hear, and value yourself on your own terms.

And these moments only get better when we know ourselves. When we love our identity. When we freely share our gifts *with* others. When we see the gifts *of* others. These moments are the ones worth living for.

Now is the time to take your Loved Identity into the world. It is a call to action to invest in knowing yourself and making space for others. Maybe it starts with reflecting on the questions introduced throughout this book at home. Or maybe it begins with a conversation with a partner or friend. The moments you take to create belonging within yourself create belonging in the world for those around you. We are all outsiders, and it's the power of creating space for those differences that unites us all.

•   •   •   •

I was talking with my daughter about how I wrote this book on belonging because I was fighting for others. She asked me if I knew what the word "fighting" meant in Korean. Confused, I said no because I had never learned the language. She shared with me that "fighting" in Korean means "to cheer someone on" and is meant as a gift of support—an act of love. In that moment I have never felt more connected to my identity as a Korean, as a mother, and to myself.

I *am* a fighter. And I am fighting for you.

You belong here.

YOU BELONG HERE

DISCUSSION GUIDE

CHAPTER 1

Describe an average day in your life. Imagine what you do from the moment you wake up until you go to sleep. Visualize the environments where those things happen.

- Where do you feel included?

- Where do you feel like an outsider?

- What are the social cues that make you feel that way?

This is a way to see opportunities for action within your environment to explore deeper when you feel like an outsider.

CHAPTER 2

Reflect on a time when you were engaging in an us-versus-them moment in your life.

- Who was the us in the story and why?

- Who was the them in the story and why?

- What was the topic of debate that put you in this us-versus-them mind-set?

Now swap roles and describe this interaction as the us *and* as the them.

- What could you do to ensure that you see a fuller picture of the them in this situation?

- What are ways that you can *call people in* versus *calling people out* in that interaction?

When we pause to leverage empathy, to fully see the context that people are bringing to a conversation, we can better engage in civil discourse and honor each other's humanity, even when we don't agree.

CHAPTER 3

Reflect on your identity and how you describe it.

- Does this description change between formal and informal settings?

- Are there circumstances where you consistently show up as your full self?

Hold that with you as we go through this Belonging Journey to see, claim, edit, and own your identity.

CHAPTER 4

The identity we inherit. The parts of us we are born with and the culture we are born into. List all of the parts of your identity that you inherited at birth. Now imagine that you are introducing yourself to a new neighbor for the first time.

- How do you respond to "Tell me about yourself"?

- Which parts of your Lived Identity are included in that introduction?

- Which parts are included if it were a new work colleague?

- Which parts are included if it were a new boss?

By seeing which parts of your identity you lead with and the parts you struggle to share, you see which aspects of your Lived Identity you hide. This allows you to better see the power and privilege others may hold within an interaction.

CHAPTER 5

Take a moment to reflect on your own origin story. Write it out as a short story and be as descriptive as possible about how your life began.

- Which parts of your Lived Identity did you claim?

- Which parts of your Lived Identity didn't show up in your origin story?

- Why is that?

Now imagine your same origin story rewritten with different aspects of a Lived Identity that weren't your own to see how they would impact your opportunities in life.

- How would your origin story change if your gender or race were different?

- How would your origin story change if you swapped out other aspects of someone else's Lived Identity?

By exploring and interrogating the systemic barriers to opportunity within the things we and others inherit, we can better understand our relationship to the things we were born with and into.

CHAPTER 6

The identity we choose. The parts of us we have claimed. You need to live your own dream, not the dream that others have defined for you. It is time to name the things in your life that you want to fight for. List ten things in your life that you care deeply about.

- Which ones do you choose to fight for?

- Who are the people you want to fight beside?

- How could that show up in your life? Your work? And your relationships?

The choices we have in life and how we claim the things we care about can be a strong guide to where we spend our time and energy. Gaining clarity on the topics that matter to us can be a consistent force in our lives.

CHAPTER 7

What are some of the guiding principles that best reflect who you are and how you show up in the world?

- Which statements guide your choices?

- Which ones do you want to amplify?

- Which ones do you want to shift?

- What are the values of those you work for and with?

- How do they align with your own values?

The more clarity we have on the things that guide the choices we make in life, the better we are able to see, hear, and value ourselves in any situation.

CHAPTER 8

The identity we default to. The old stories we tell ourselves about who we are and what we deserve. The myth of *I'm too this or that* is a hard one to break. To reset these stories, you first have to know where they show up over and over in your life.

- What are the I'm *too this or that* stories you tell yourself?

- When do they show up?

- What are the situations or triggers before your inner voice says I'm *too this or that?*

I have my own three questions I ask myself in the moments when my Lingering Identity shows up. Now design your own three questions that you can ask yourself that provide you with the space to reclaim agency and respond authentically.

CHAPTER 9

Introduce yourself to yourself as if you were your own biggest fan.

- What would your biggest fan say about you?

- How would they describe you?

- What qualities would they highlight?

Your biggest fan may just find that your *I'm too this or that* stories that you used to see as your kryptonite could be your superpower.

CHAPTER 10

Our authentic identity. The power of being seen, heard, and valued on our own terms. A motto I carry with me in my own life is "You Belong Here." Create your own motto about who you are and how your Loved Identity shows up in the world.

- When you read through your motto, does it make your heart skip a beat?

- Do you feel it in your bones?

Now take inventory of the interactions and choices you made when you owned your Loved Identity and felt that you showed up as your authentic self.

- What are the words that you would describe yourself as in these instances?

- In your workplace teams what are the moments where you were able to come as you are?

- In your community what are the situations where you felt valued for just being you?

Look for the patterns that emerge and take that into the world through your words and actions.

CHAPTER 11

Take a moment to think about a time when people gather in your life. Maybe it is a meeting at work or a dinner with a loved one.

- How might you leverage the power of rituals to build a new table together?

- What is a quick way to redesign gatherings with them?

- When you are invited to a table that wasn't set for you, what are three questions you can ask to ensure you can come as you are?

Designing a filter check through these three questions, you have something to ground yourself in that you can either hold close or share to ensure you belong to yourself in any situation.

NOTES

INTRODUCTION

1. Geoff MacDonald and Mark R. Leary, "Why Does Social Exclusion Hurt? The Relationship Between Social and Physical Pain," *Psychological Bulletin* 131, no. 2 (2005): 202–223, https://doi.org/10.1037/0033-2909.131.2.202.

CHAPTER 1

2. MacDonald and Leary, "Why Does Social Exclusion Hurt?"
3. Naomi I. Eisenberger, Matthew D. Lieberman, and Kipling D. Williams, "Does Rejection Hurt? An FMRI Study of Social Exclusion," *Science* 302, no. 5643 (2003): 290–292, https://doi.org/10.1126/science.1089134.
4. Arline T. Geronimus, "The Physical Toll Systemic Injustice Takes on the Body," *Time*, March 28, 2023, https://time.com/6266329/systemic-injustice-health-toll-weathering/. The article is adapted from her book *Weathering: The Extraordinary Stress of Ordinary Life on the Body in an Unjust Society* (London: Little, Brown, 2023).
5. Geronimus, "Physical Toll Systemic Injustice Takes."
6. Ruchika Tulshyan and Jodi-Ann Burey, "Stop Telling Women They Have Imposter Syndrome," *Harvard Business Review*, February 11, 2021, https://hbr.org/2021/02/stop-telling-women-they-have-imposter-syndrome.
7. Maggie De Pree, interview with the author, May 2023.

CHAPTER 2

8. Linda Darling-Hammond, "Unequal Opportunity: Race and Education," Brookings, March 1, 1998, https://www.brookings.edu/articles/unequal-opportunity-race-and-education/.

9. Elizabeth Ferris, "When Refugee Displacement Drags on, Is Self-reliance the Answer?," Brookings, June 19, 2018, https://www.brookings.edu/articles/when-refugee-displacement-drags-on-is-self-reliance-the-answer/.

10. Daniel Wordsworth, interview with the author, December 2022.

11. Siyu Lu, Fang Wei, and Guolin Li, "The Evolution of the Concept of Stress and the Framework of the Stress System," *Cell Stress* 5, no. 6 (2021): 76–85, DOI: 10.15698/cst2021.06.250.

12. "Neuroscience and How Students Learn," GSI Teaching & Research Center, accessed July 13, 2023, https://gsi.berkeley.edu/gsi-guide-contents/learning-theory-research/neuroscience/.

13. Matthew Dixon, "Does the Amygdala Hijack Your Brain?," *Psychology Today*, January 3, 2023, https://www.psychologytoday.com/intl/blog/202301/does-the-amygdala-hijack-your-brain.

CHAPTER 3

14. Shahram Heshmat, "Basics of Identity," *Psychology Today*, December 8, 2014, https://www.psychologytoday.com/us/blog/science-choice/201412/basics-identity.

CHAPTER 4

15. Bill Leonard, "Study Suggests Bias Against 'Black' Names on Resumes," *HR Magazine*, February 1, 2003, https://www.shrm.org/hr-today/news/hr-magazine/pages/0203hrnews2.aspx.

16. Yodit Mesfin Johnson, interview with the author, May 2023.

CHAPTER 5

17. Steve Haruch, "In Korea, Adoptees Fight to Change Culture That Sent Them Overseas," *NPR*, September 9, 2014, https://www.npr.org/sections/codeswitch/2014/09/09/346851939/in-korea-adoptees-fight-to-change-culture-that-sent-them-overseas.

CHAPTER 6

18. NBER research as cited in Sarah Kliff, Claire Cain Miller, and Larry Buchanan, "Childbirth Is Deadlier for Black Families Even When They're Rich, Expansive Study Finds," *New York Times*, March 13, 2023, https://www.nytimes.com/interactive/2023/02/12/upshot/child-maternal-mortality-rich-poor.html.

19. Alissa Quart, "Bootstrapping Has Always Been a Myth. The New American Dream Proves It," *Time*, March 10, 2023, https://time.com/6261476/bootstrapping-myth-new-american-dream/, adaptation of *Bootstrapped: Liberating Ourselves from the American Dream* (New York: Harper Collins, 2023).

20. Kinga Pakucs, interview with the author, April 2023.

21. Alexandra Moldovan, interview with the author, April 2023.

CHAPTER 7

22. Jesse McKinley, "A Changing Battle on AIDS Is Reflected in a Quilt," *New York Times*, January 31, 2007, https://www.nytimes.com/2007/01/31/us/31quilt.html.

23. Paulo Freire, *The Pedagogy of the Oppressed: 50th Anniversary Edition*, translated by Myra B. Ramos (New York: Bloomsbury Academic, 2018), 44.

24. Brené Brown, "Brené on Shame and Accountability," July 2020, podcast *Unlocking Us with Brené Brown*, produced by Cadence13, https://brenebrown.com/podcast/brene-on-shame-and-accountability/.

CHAPTER 8

25. Tchiki Davis, "6 Ways to Calm Your Fight-or-Flight Response," *Psychology Today*, August 16, 2021, https://www.psychologytoday.com/intl/blog/click-here-happiness/202108/6-ways-calm-your-fight-or-flight-response.

26. Harvard Medical School, "Understanding the Stress Response," *Harvard Health Publishing*, July 6, 2020, https://www.health.harvard.edu/staying-healthy/understanding-the-stress-response.

27. Matt Puderbaugh and Prabhu D. Emmady, "Neuroplasticity," *StatPearls*, May 1, 2023, https://www.ncbi.nlm.nih.gov/books /NBK557811/.

28. Christopher Bergland as quoted in Courtney E. Ackerman, "What Is Neuroplasticity? A Psychologist Explains [+14 Tools]," *PositivePsychology.com*, July 25, 2018, https://positivepsychology.com /neuroplasticity/.

29. Traci Pedersen, "What Are Triggers, and How Do They Form?," *Psych Central*, April 28, 2022, https://psychcentral.com/lib/what-is -a-trigger.

30. Emily Bashforth, "Managing PTSD during Fireworks Season," *Patient*, November 1, 2021, https://patient.info/news-and-features /managing-ptsd-during-fireworks-season.

CHAPTER 9

31. Ti Chang, interview with the author, May 2023.

32. Trabian Shorters, "'You Can't Lift People Up by Putting Them Down': How to Talk about Tough Issues of Race, Poverty, and More," *Chronicle of Philanthropy*, June 26, 2019, https://www.philanthropy.com /article/you-cant-lift-people-up-by-putting-them-down-how-to-talk-about -tough-issues-of-race-poverty-and-more.

33. Chang, interview.

CHAPTER 10

34. Shannon Cohen, interview with the author, May 2023.

35. Janice Gassam Asare, "How Hair Discrimination Affects Black Women at Work," *Harvard Business Review*, May 10, 2023, https://hbr .org/2023/05/how-hair-discrimination-affects-black-women-at-work.

36. Cohen, interview.

CHAPTER 11

37. Roy F. Baumeister and Mark R. Leary, "The Need to Belong: Desire for Interpersonal Attachments as a Fundamental Human

Motivation," *Psychological Bulletin* 117, no. 3 (1995): 497–529, https://doi
.org/10.1037/0033-2909.117.3.497.

38. Juliet Eilperin, "White House Women Want to Be in the Room
Where It Happens," *Washington Post,* September 13, 2016, https://www
.washingtonpost.com/news/powerpost/wp/2016/09/13/white-house
-women-are-now-in-the-room-where-it-happens/.

39. Susan Chira, "The Universal Phenomenon of Men Interrupting
Women," *New York Times,* June 15, 2017, https://www.nytimes.com
/2017/06/14/business/women-sexism-work-huffington-kamala-harris
.html. Jason Maderer, "Women Interrupted: A New Strategy for Male-
Dominated Discussions," Carnegie Mellon University, October 21, 2020,
https://www.cmu.edu/news/stories/archives/2020/october/women
-interrupted-debate.html.

40. Allaya Cooks-Campbell, "Code-switching: More Common Than
You Think and Hurting Your Team," *Better Up,* March 1, 2022, https://
www.betterup.com/blog/code-switching.

41. Beca Velásquez-Publes, interview with the author, May 2023.

42. "We Are Alight," Alight, accessed July 17, 2023, https://
wearealight.org/.

43. Bernad Ochieng Ojwang, interview with the author, February
2022.

CONCLUSION

44. Claire E. Oppenheim, "Nelson Mandela and the Power of
Ubuntu," *Religions* 3, no. 2 (2012): 369–388, https://doi.org/10.3390
/rel3020369.

RECOMMENDED READING

Allen, Kelly-Ann. 2020. *The Psychology of Belonging*. London: Routledge, Taylor & Francis Group.

Bacon, Lindo. 2020. *Radical Belonging: How to Survive and Thrive in an Unjust World (While Transforming It for the Better)*. Dallas, TX: BenBella Books.

Block, Peter. 2018. *Community: The Structure of Belonging*. Oakland, CA: Berrett-Koehler Publishers.

Cohen, Geoffrey L. 2022. *Belonging: The Science of Creating Connection and Bridging Divides*. New York: WW Norton.

Freire, Paulo. 2018. *Pedagogy of the Oppressed: 50th Anniversary Edition*. Translated by Myra B. Ramos. New York: Bloomsbury Academic.

Geronimus, Arline. 2023. *Weathering: The Extraordinary Stress of Ordinary Life on the Body in an Unjust Society*. London: Little, Brown Book Group Limited.

Gladwell, Malcolm. 2011. *Outliers: The Story of Success*. New York: Penguin Group.

hooks, bell. 2009. *Belonging: A Culture of Place*. New York: Routledge.

Jacob, Kathryn, Mark Edwards, and Sue Unerman. 2020. *Belonging: The Key to Transforming and Maintaining Diversity, Inclusion and Equality at Work*. Dublin: Bloomsbury.

May, Vanessa. 2013. *Connecting Self to Society: Belonging in a Changing World*. London: Macmillan Education UK.

Mortensen, Peter, and Dev Patnaik. 2009. *Wired to Care: How Companies Prosper When They Create Widespread Empathy*. Upper Saddle River, NJ: FT Press.

Selasi, Taiye. 2014. "Don't Ask Where I'm From, Ask Where I'm a Local." *TED*. https://www.ted.com/talks/taiye_selasi_don _t_ask_where_i_m_from_ask_where_i_m_a_local/transcript ?language=en.

Shorters, Trabian. 2023. *Website of Trabian Shorters Thought Leader and Creator of Asset-Framing®*. https://trabianshorters.com/.

Taylor, Sonya Renee. 2021. *The Body Is Not an Apology: The Power of Radical Self-Love*. Second edition. Oakland, CA: Berrett-Koehler Publishers.

Wise, Susie, and Stanford d.school. 2022. *Design for Belonging: How to Build Inclusion and Collaboration in Your Communities*. Berkeley: Clarkson Potter/Ten Speed.

ACKNOWLEDGMENTS

Thank you to the entire Berrett-Koehler team for believing in belonging. To Steve Piersanti, my editor, for being a coach, mentor, and friend. I have learned so much through this process, and your patience and compassion has made this book, and me, better. To Katelyn Keating, for your guidance, as we both learned through this new adventure. Your feedback has been a gift. And to Ashley Ingram and the design team for seeing, hearing, and valuing my vision for this book and for bringing my words to life through visuals. You are one of the best creative directors and teams I've ever worked with.

I couldn't have written this book without the collaboration and care of Michael Thompson. Your support and guidance on this journey have brought this book and movement to life in so many different ways.

All of these stories would not have been possible without Beca Velázquez-Publes, Shannon Cohen, Maggie De Pree, Yodit Mesfin Johnson, Ti Chang, Daniel Wordsworth, Bernad Ochieng Ojwang, Kinga Pakucs, and Alexandra Moldovan graciously sharing their own journeys to belonging. Your strength and care have inspired us all.

As the To Belonging movement was launched, it wouldn't have been possible without the collaboration of a team of friends in random cities and mountain cabins over these past couple of years. Thank you, Yuen Hom, Pilar Marín Legaz, Karen Saukas, Kinga Pakucs, Alexandra Moldovan, Elena De Kan, and Hristina Bojkova, for being the people you are.

To my board of experts who have been my guides as I jumped into a whole new industry: Roshi Givechi, Christine Lai, Tony Bond, Ada Williams Prince, John Abodeely, and David Cleaves. Thank you for your wisdom.

And to Steelcase, a big thank you for bringing belonging to the forefront of our values and strategy. The company has made people and our planet a priority for ourselves and the world. Aileen Strickland McGee and Kim Koeman, thank you for your leadership and the ways you have been there for me as I balanced these two parts of my life.

My family is my home. No matter where we are in the world, I know wherever they are, I am loved. To my husband, Steve, and our kids, Micah, Henry, and Olive: this book is a love letter to you and for you. I want the world we live in and the world you grow up in to be one where you have the courage and confidence to love who you are. Because you, my loves, are perfect. Thank you for building a life together and creating the space for me to be me.

And to all of you reading this book, thank you for believing that change is possible.

INDEX

Page numbers followed by an *f* indicate a figure.

Adoption. *See* South Korean children
AIDS Memorial Quilt, 89–90
American Civil Liberties Union
    (ACLU), 90–91
"Amplification" pact, 143–145
Assisters and resisters, 84
Autopilot, your brain on, 104–106

"Be for each other" (Hatch), 97
Belonging. *See also* Belonging to
    yourself; *specific topics*
    begins with you, 4–7
    etymology of the term, viii, 17
    I don't belong here, 16, 128
    from inclusion to, 15–18, 36–37
    nature of, viii, 3
    not belonging hurts, 18–22
    questions for getting rooted in,
        109–111
    the search for, 33–37
    You belong here, 6, 11, 127, 130, 136,
        137, 153, 156
Belonging conversation, 16
Belonging Journey, 7–8, 10, 92, 93, 98,
    111, 155
    beginning of, 52, 67
    build to belong, 67, 69–70

Dabbs's, 67, 92–93, 108, 155
    gifts of going on, 103, 108, 138, 142,
        145, 155
    overview, 45, 45f
    reasons for going on, 67, 108, 158
    steps in, 45–49, 72, 109, 123, 126, 127.
        See also Identities
Belonging retreats (BEtreats), 152–153
Belonging to yourself, 84–87. *See also*
    Belonging
    and discovering others, 136,
        138–139
    is a revolutionary act, 132–136
Bergland, Christopher, 105
BEtreats (belonging retreats), 152–153
Bias(es), 32, 96
    impact, 32–33, 74, 96
    loops of, 104, 105
    overcoming, 84, 105
    seeing, 84, 96
Black women, 74, 132, 133
Brain. *See* Neuroscience
Bravery, acting with, 95–96
Building a new table, 127, 128, 139, 145,
    147–148
    overview, 142, 151
    a table set for everyone, 143–145

Calling people in vs. calling people
    out, 41
Camp Ignite, 79, 80, 82
Chang, Ti, 113–116, 119–120, 128
Code-switching, 145–146
Cohen, Shannon, 132–135
"Corporate," being, 76
COVID-19 pandemic, 119, 154
Cultural identity. *See* Korean identity
Culture(s), 5, 24
    building/creating a culture of
        belonging, 5, 6, 17–18, 33, 98,
        126, 149
    oppressed, 36. *See also* Oppression
    organizational, 25

Day in your life, describing an average,
    27
De Pree, Maggie, 26
Diversity, equity, and inclusion (DEI),
    4–5
"Do or do not, there is no try" (Yoda),
    96–97

Ego, impact over, 96
Eilperin, Juliet, 143–144
Ethnic identity. *See* Korean identity
Exclusion, experience(s) of, 40, 55, 57
    compared with physical pain, 3, 21
    Dabbs's, 2, 3, 17, 19
    efforts to alleviate, 23
    shift to inclusion and belonging,
        15–18, 36–37
    Ti Chang's, 114–116
    understanding, 10, 15, 17, 49

Fight, flight, freeze, or fawn responses,
    13, 39

"Fighting," meanings of the term, 156
Forever work, 7, 17, 132

Geronimus, Arline, 22
Gifts, 138
    buried/hidden, 35, 83, 117
    Dabbs's, 52, 98
    identifying, 35, 49, 79, 84, 117, 119,
        127
    sharing, 35, 95, 98, 119, 127, 131, 142,
        155, 156
GLOW Camp (Girls Leading Our
    World), 78, 80, 81
Guiding principles
    design your, 92–100
    your own, 99

HIV/AIDS, 89–90
Homecoming Day, 58
Humanity, responding with, 111

"I am here to get it right, not to be
    right" (Brown), 98
I don't belong here, 16, 128. *See also You
    belong here*
Identities, four, 45. *See also* Learned
    Identity; Lingering Identity; Lived
    Identity; Loved Identity
    belonging within our, 7–11
    overview, 8–10, 44
Identity. *See also* Korean identity
    reflecting on your, 48
I'm not that stories, 104–105, 111, 112,
    115, 122
    Dabbs's, 2, 106
I'm too this stories, 104–105, 110–112,
    115, 121, 122
    Dabbs's, 2, 11, 106, 120

Ti Chang's, 115, 119, 120, 128
Impact over ego, 96
Inclusion. *See also under* Belonging;
    Exclusion
    diversity, equity, and, 4–5

Johnson, Yodit Mesfin, 55–57, 127–128
Jones, Cleve, 89–90

Korean American, experiences of
    being, 66. *See also* South Korea
    Dabbs's, 1, 2, 10, 11, 13, 51–52, 60, 66
Korean identity. *See also* South Korea
    Dabbs's, 10, 51, 52, 57, 58, 60, 66,
        67, 156

League of Intrapreneurs, 26
Learned Identity, 72
    challenging norms, 77–81
    claiming your, 9, 47, 72–77, 85
    defined, 8, 44
    nature of, 9, 47
    your own dream, 81–83
Leary, Mark, 21
Lifestyle. *See* Day in your life
Lingering Identity
    defined, 8, 44
    editing your, 9, 47, 102–104, 110
    nature of, 9–10, 47
Lived Identity
    defined, 8, 44
    nature of, 8–9, 46–47
    seeing your, 8, 46, 52–55, 59
Loved Identity, 11, 125–126. *See also*
    Belonging to yourself
    defined, 8, 44
    nature of, 10–11, 48
    owning our, 10, 48, 126–129, 137

MacDonald, Geoff, 21
Mandela, Nelson, 153–154
Marriage equality, 36
Me, from we to, 37–40
Microaggressions, 14, 101. *See also*
    "Sharp elbows"
Moldovan, Alexandra, 77–83, 128

NAMES Project's AIDS Memorial
    Quilt, 89–90
Narrative, rewriting your, 115–119
Neuroplasticity, 105
Neuroscience, 38, 39, 103–105
New table. *See* Building a new table

Obama, Barack, 143–144
Ojwang, Bernad Ochieng, 150
Oppression, 35–36, 94. *See also*
    Refugee camps
    systems of, 31, 74
Organizational culture, 25
Origin story, 52, 62, 67, 69, 86, 98,
    146
    Belonging Journey and, 52, 67
    build to belong, 67, 69–70
    Dabbs's, 51–52, 62–67, 64f. *See also*
        South Korea: Dabbs's experi-
        ences in
    homecoming, 62–67
    knowing your, 52
    Lived Identity and, 68
    understanding your, 73, 126
    what we inherit, 62
    writing your, 67, 68
Orphans. *See* South Korean children
Othering, 22. *See also* Us vs. them

Pakucs, Kinga, 77, 79–83, 128

Passive-aggressive jabs. *See* "Sharp
    elbows"
Peace Corps, 78, 81
Philanthropy, 118
Polarization, 31
Post-traumatic stress disorder (PTSD),
    107–108. *See also* Triggers
Powell, John, 56
Power
    speaking truth to, 94
    using power to share, 94–95
Pressing reset, 111–112
Productive tension, 39
"Professionalism," 24–26
    not being "professional" enough,
        24, 26, 36, 111
Protection mode, 104, 109. *See also*
    Survival mode

Racism, 54–56. *See also* Black women;
    Korean American
Refugee camps, 34–35
Reset, pressing, 111–112
Resisters and assisters, 84
Rituals and norms, 148–152
Romania, 77–82
Royal Academy of Arts in London
    (RCA), 115

Safe spaces, 33, 134
    belonging and, 11, 17, 145–148
    creating, 17, 82–83, 100, 142,
        144–145
    identity and, 6
    meanings of the term, 145
    nature of, 5, 145
Safety, 109

Sameness, algorithm of, 23–25
Self-reflection. *See* Identity
"Sharp elbows" (passive-aggressive
    jabs), 135
Shorters, Trabian, 117–118
South Korea, 66. *See also* Korean
    American; Korean identity
    Dabbs's experiences in, 1, 13, 15,
        60–66, 64f. *See also* Origin
        story: Dabbs's
South Korean children, international
    adoption of, 58, 62–63. *See also*
    under South Korea
Speaking truth to power, 94
Standing on our own, 129–131
Star Wars, 96–97
Stories, sunsetting old, 103, 116, 122
    and editing your Lingering Identity,
        155
    overview, 121
    steps in the process of, 10, 47, 103,
        105–108, 112
Survival mechanism(s), 20
    falling back into default as, 9. *See
        also* Lingering Identity
Survival mode, 13, 21, 103, 104. *See also*
    Protection mode

Table, new. *See* Building a new table
"Too's," retiring your, 120–123
Trauma, 104–105, 107–108. *See also*
    Refugee camps
    healing, 105
Triggers, 38. *See also* Fight, flight,
    freeze ,or fawn responses
    Dabbs's, 9–10, 61, 101, 106–109
    defined, 107

identifying, 10, 47, 103, 105,
   107–112
and response, 106–111
words as, 61
Truth, speaking, 94

Ubuntu philosophy, 153–154
Us vs. them, 76, 89, 94. *See also*
   Othering
defining your us and them, 41
the illusion of, 31–33
vs. inclusion, 36

us-vs.-them cultures, 31–33, 53
us-vs.-them cycle, 143

Values, claiming your, 91–92
Velázquez-Publes, Beca, 146–148

We to me, from, 37–40
Weathering (Geronimus), 22
Wordsworth, Daniel, 33–35, 37, 40, 127

You belong here, 6, 11, 127, 130, 136, 137,
   153; 156. *See also I don't belong here*

ABOUT THE AUTHOR

 **Kim Dabbs** is a global leader in the area of belonging and purpose. For the past two decades, her work—spanning both the nonprofit and corporate sector in the United States and abroad—has focused on helping individuals, team leaders, organizations, and communities gain the tools to create a more equitable and inclusive world.

Kim has given talks on identity and building cultures of belonging at such organizations as TEDx, the Massachusetts Institute of Technology, the Aspen Institute, the Drucker Forum, the Equity Lounge at the World Economic Forum, and the Guggenheim. She has received numerous recognitions throughout her career. These include a Joyce Fellowship from Americans for the Arts, a three-month residency at Stanford's d.school with leadership training in human-centered design, and being selected as an innovation coach at IDEO U. While serving as the executive director of the West Michigan Center for Arts and Technology (WMCAT), Kim and her team crafted a new model rooted in holistic belonging for both adult career training and teen arts + tech engagement, leading to WMCAT's recognition by the White House as a national best practice.

Kim currently serves as the global vice president of ESG (environmental, social, and governance) and social innovation at Steelcase, a global design firm and thought leader in the future of work. For more than a century, Steelcase has designed, manufactured, and partnered with the world's leading organizations to create furnishings and solutions for the many places where work happens. Kim leads the organization in setting a bold global ESG strategy to build a more sustainable, inclusive, and equitable world. She works with the executive leaders of their global clients and communities to design cultural transformation projects investing in social impact initiatives where they live and work to ensure long-term impact.

During the seven years Kim has been part of the executive team, Steelcase continues to lead the industry in practices for people and the planet, earning a perfect 100-point score on the Corporate Equality Index issued by the Human Rights Campaign. In addition, Steelcase has been named as one of the top fifty community-minded companies by the Points of Light foundation, recognized by *Forbes* as one of the Best Employers for Women, and named as one of the World's Most Admired Companies by *Fortune* magazine.

Prior to joining Steelcase, Kim led nonprofit organizations in the equity, education, and public policy spaces. The longer she experienced barriers to progress for the organizations and the people she served, the more she wanted to work at scale within the systems that she saw as the root cause of·many of these systemic barriers. At Steelcase, Kim leverages business as a force for good by mobilizing the organization's 12,000 employees, 770 dealership locations, and more than three billion dollars in annual revenue to point the future toward the wellbeing of people and the planet to help the world work better. She currently lives in Munich, Germany, with her family.

ABOUT TO BELONGING

The organization To Belonging believes that everyone deserves to be seen, heard, and valued in the identity they love. Through an exploration of identity and culture, To Belonging is building a community that creates safe spaces at home, work, and in the community where everyone can thrive. It supports the work of exploring ourselves and our purpose through workshops, speeches, and retreats around the world. Belonging is realized when we understand everyone is an outsider, and it's the power of creating space for those differences that unites us all. Join the revolution at tobelonging.com.

BK Berrett–Koehler
Publishers

Berrett-Koehler is an independent publisher dedicated to an ambitious mission: *Connecting people and ideas to create a world that works for all.*

Our publications span many formats, including print, digital, audio, and video. We also offer online resources, training, and gatherings. And we will continue expanding our products and services to advance our mission.

We believe that the solutions to the world's problems will come from all of us, working at all levels: in our society, in our organizations, and in our own lives. Our publications and resources offer pathways to creating a more just, equitable, and sustainable society. They help people make their organizations more humane, democratic, diverse, and effective (and we don't think there's any contradiction there). And they guide people in creating positive change in their own lives and aligning their personal practices with their aspirations for a better world.

And we strive to practice what we preach through what we call "The BK Way." At the core of this approach is *stewardship,* a deep sense of responsibility to administer the company for the benefit of all of our stakeholder groups, including authors, customers, employees, investors, service providers, sales partners, and the communities and environment around us. Everything we do is built around stewardship and our other core values of *quality, partnership, inclusion,* and *sustainability.*

This is why Berrett-Koehler is the first book publishing company to be both a B Corporation (a rigorous certification) and a benefit corporation (a for-profit legal status), which together require us to adhere to the highest standards for corporate, social, and environmental performance. And it is why we have instituted many pioneering practices (which you can learn about at www.bkconnection.com), including the Berrett-Koehler Constitution, the Bill of Rights and Responsibilities for BK Authors, and our unique Author Days.

We are grateful to our readers, authors, and other friends who are supporting our mission. We ask you to share with us examples of how BK publications and resources are making a difference in your lives, organizations, and communities at www.bkconnection.com/impact.

Dear reader,

Thank you for picking up this book and welcome to the worldwide BK community! You're joining a special group of people who have come together to create positive change in their lives, organizations, and communities.

What's BK all about?

Our mission is to connect people and ideas to create a world that works for all.

Why? Our communities, organizations, and lives get bogged down by old paradigms of self-interest, exclusion, hierarchy, and privilege. But we believe that can change. That's why we seek the leading experts on these challenges—and share their actionable ideas with you.

A welcome gift

To help you get started, we'd like to offer you a **free copy** of one of our bestselling ebooks:

www.bkconnection.com/welcome

When you claim your **free ebook**, you'll also be subscribed to our blog.

Our freshest insights

Access the best new tools and ideas for leaders at all levels on our blog at ideas.bkconnection.com.

Sincerely,

Your friends at Berrett-Koehler